The Letters of Ambrose Bierce

The
Letters of Ambrose Bierce

EDITED BY

BERTHA CLARK POPE

WITH A MEMOIR BY

GEORGE STERLING

GORDIAN PRESS

New York

1967

Originally Published 1922
Reprinted 1967

Library of Congress Catalogue Card Number 67-30702

Published by GORDIAN PRESS

The Introduction
by BERTHA CLARK POPE

The Introduction

by BERTHA CLARK POPE

"THE *question that starts to the lips of ninety-nine read-ers out of a hundred," says Arnold Bennett, in a re-view in the London* NEW AGE *in 1909, "even the best informed, will assuredly be: 'Who is Ambrose Bierce?' I scarcely know, but I will say that among what I may term 'underground reputations' that of Ambrose Bierce is per-haps the most striking example. You may wander for years through literary circles and never meet anybody who has heard of Ambrose Bierce, and then you may hear some eru-dite student whisper in an awed voice: 'Ambrose Bierce is the greatest living prose writer.' I have heard such an opin-ion expressed."*

Bierce himself shows his recognition of the "underground" quality of his reputation in a letter to George Sterling: "How many times, and during a period of how many years must one's unexplainable obscurity be pointed out to constitute fame? Not knowing, I am almost disposed to consider my-self the most famous of authors. I have pretty nearly ceased to be 'discovered,' but my notoriety as an obscurian may be said to be worldwide and everlasting."

Anything which would throw light on such a figure, at once

*obscure and famous, is valuable. These letters of Ambrose
Bierce, here printed for the first time, are therefore of unu-
sual interest. They are the informal literary work—the term
is used advisedly—of a man esteemed great by a small but
acutely critical group, read enthusiastically by a somewhat
larger number to whom critical examination of what they
read seldom occurs, and ignored by the vast majority of readers; a man at once more hated and more adored than any on
the Pacific Coast; a man not ten years off the scene yet already
become a tradition and a legend; whose life, no less than his
death, held elements of mystery, baffling contradictions, problems for puzzled conjecture, motives and meanings not
vouchsafed to outsiders.*

   *Were Ambrose Bierce as well known as he deserves to be,
the introduction to these letters could be slight; we should not
have to stop to inquire who he was and what he did. As it is,
we must.*

   *Ambrose Bierce, the son of Marcus Aurelius and Laura
(Sherwood) Bierce, born in Meiggs County, Ohio, June 24,
1842, was at the outbreak of the Civil War a youth without formal education, but with a mind already trained. "My
father was a poor farmer," he once said to a friend, "and
could give me no general education, but he had a good library, and to his books I owe all that I have." He promptly vol-
unteered in 1861 and served throughout the war. Twice, at
the risk of his life, he rescued wounded companions from the
battlefield, and at Kenesaw Mountain was himself severely
wounded in the head. He was brevetted Major for distin-*

guished services, but in after life never permitted the title to be used in addressing him. There is a story that when the war was over he tossed up a coin to determine what should be his career. Whatever the determining auguries, he came at once to San Francisco to join his favorite brother Albert—there were ten brothers and sisters to choose from—and for a short time worked with him in the Mint; he soon began writing paragraphs for the weeklies, particularly the ARGONAUT and the NEWS LETTER.

"I was a slovenly writer in those days," he observes in a letter forty years later, "though enough better than my neighbors to have attracted my own attention. My knowledge of English was imperfect 'a whole lot.' Indeed, my intellectual status (whatever it may be, and God knows it's enough to make me blush) was of slow growth—as was my moral. I mean, I had not literary sincerity." Apparently, attention other than his own was attracted, for he was presently editing the NEWS LETTER.

In 1872 he went to London and for four years was on the staff of FUN. In London Bierce found congenial and stimulating associates. The great man of his circle was George Augustus Sala, "one of the most skilful, finished journalists ever known," a keen satiric wit, and the author of a ballad of which it is said that Swift might have been proud. Another notable figure was Tom Hood the younger, mordantly humorous. The satiric style in journalism was popular then; and "personal" journals were so personal that one "Jimmy" Davis, editor of the CUCKOO and the BAT successively,

*found it healthful to remain some years in exile in France.
Bierce contributed to several of these and to* FIGARO, *the
editor of which was James Mortimer. To this gentleman
Bierce owed what he designated as the distinction of being
"probably the only American journalist who was ever employed by an Empress in so congenial a pursuit as the pursuit of another journalist." This other journalist was M.
Henri Rochefort, communard, formerly editor of* LA LAN-
TERNE *in Paris, in which he had made incessant war upon
the Empire and all its personnel, particularly the Empress.
When, an exile, Rochefort announced his intention of re-
newing* LA LANTERNE *in London, the exiled Empress
circumvented him by secretly copyrighting the title,* THE
LANTERN, *and proceeding to publish a periodical under
that name with the purpose of undermining his influence.
Two numbers were enough; M. Rochefort fled to Belgium.
Bierce said that in "the field of chromatic journalism" it
was the finest thing that ever came from a press, but of the
literary excellence of the twelve pages he felt less qualified
for judgment as he had written every line.*

*This was in 1874. Two years earlier, under his journal-
istic pseudonym of "Dod Grile," he had published his first
books—two small volumes, largely made up of his articles
in the San Francisco* NEWS LETTER, *called* The Fiend's
Delight, *and* Nuggets And Dust Panned Out In California. *Now, he used the same pseudonym on the title-page of
a third volume,* Cobwebs from an Empty Skull. *The*
Cobwebs *were selections from his work in* FUN—*satirical*

tales and fables, often inspired by weird old woodcuts given
him by the editors with the request that he write something
to fit. His journalistic associates praised these volumes liber-
ally, and a more distinguished admirer was Gladstone, who,
discovering the Cobwebs in a second-hand bookshop, voiced
his delight in their cleverness, and by his praise gave a certain currency to Bierce's name among the London elect. But
despite so distinguished a sponsor, the books remained generally unknown.

Congenial tasks and association with the brilliant joural-
ists of the day did not prevent Bierce from being undeniably
hard up at times. In 1876 he returned to San Francisco,
where he remained for twenty-one years, save for a brief
but eventful career as general manager of a mining company near Deadwood, South Dakota. All this time he got his
living by writing special articles—for the WASP, a weekly
whose general temper may be accurately surmised from its
name, and, beginning in 1886, for the EXAMINER, in which
he conducted every Sunday on the editorial page a department to which he gave the title he had used for a similar column in THE LANTERN—Prattle. A partial explanation
of a mode of feeling and a choice of themes which Bierce de-
veloped more and more, ultimately to the pratical exclusion
of all others, is to be found in the particular phase through
which California journalism was just then passing.

In the evolution of the comic spirit the lowest stage, that of
delight in inflicting pain on others, is clearly manifest in savages, small boys, and early American journalism. It was ex-

hibited in all parts of America—Mark Twain gives a vivid example in his Journalistic Wild Oats of what it was in Tennessee—but with particular intensity in San Francisco. As a community, San Francisco exalted personal courage, directness of encounter, straight and effective shooting. The social group was so small and so homogeneous that any news of importance would be well known before it could be reported, set up in type, printed, and circulated. It was isolated by so great distances from the rest of the world that for years no pretense was made of furnishing adequate news from the outside. So the newspapers came to rely on other sorts of interest. They were pamphlets for the dissemination of the opinions of the groups controlling them, and weapons for doing battle, if need be, for those opinions. And there was abundant occasion: municipal affairs were corrupt, courts weak or venal, or both. Editors and readers enjoyed a good fight; they also wanted humorous entertainment; they happily combined the two. In the creative dawn of 1847 when the foundations of the journalistic earth were laid and those two morning stars, the CALIFORNIAN of Monterey and the CALIFORNIA STAR of San Francisco, sang together, we find the editors attacking the community generally, and each other particularly, with the utmost ferocity, laying about them right and left with verbal broad-axes, crow-bars, and such other weapons as might be immediately at hand. The CALIFORNIA STAR's introduction to the public of what would, in our less direct day, be known as its "esteemed contemporary" is typical:

"*We have received two late numbers of the* CALIFORNIAN, *a dim, dirty little paper printed in Monterey on the worn-out materials of one of the old California* WAR PRESSES. *It is published and edited by Walter Colton and Robert Semple, the one a* WHINING SYCOPHANT, *and the other an* OVER-GROWN LICK-SPITTLE. *At the top of one of the papers we find the words 'please exchange.' This would be considered in almost any other country a bare-faced attempt to swindle us. We should consider it so now were it not for the peculiar situation of our country which induces us to do a great deal for others in order for them to do us a little good. . . . We have concluded to give our paper to them this year, so as to afford them some insight into the manner in which a Republican newspaper should be conducted. They appear now to be awfully verdant.*"

Down through the seventies and eighties the tradition persisted, newspapers being bought and read, as a historian of journalism asserts, not so much for news as to see who was getting "lambasted" that day. It is not strange, then, that journals of redoubtable pugnacity were popular, or that editors favored writers who were likely to excel in the gladiatorial style. It is significant that public praise first came to Bierce through his articles in the caustic NEWS LETTER, *widely read on the Pacific Coast during the seventies. Once launched in this line, he became locally famous for his fierce and witty articles in the* ARGONAUT *and the* WASP, *and for many years his column* Prattle *in the* EXAMINER *was, in the words of Mr. Bailey Millard, "the most wickedly clever, the most audaciously personal, and the most eagerly devoured column of* causerie *that ever was printed in this country.*"

In 1896 Bierce was sent to Washington to fight, through the Hearst newspapers, the "refunding bill" which Collis P. Huntington was trying to get passed, releasing his Central Pacific Railroad from its obligations to the government. A year later he went again to Washington, where he remained during the rest of his journalistic career, as correspondent for the New York AMERICAN, *conducting also for some years a department in the* COSMOPOLITAN.

Much of Bierce's best work was done in those years in San Francisco. Through the columns of the WASP *and the* EXAMINER *his wit played free; he wielded an extraordinary influence; his trenchant criticism made and unmade reputations—literary and otherwise. But this to Bierce was mostly "journalism, a thing so low that it cannot be mentioned in the same breath with literature." His real interest lay elsewhere. Throughout the early eighties he devoted himself to writing stories; all were rejected by the magazine editors to whom he offered them. When finally in 1890 he gathered these stories together into book form and offered them to the leading publishers of the country, they too, would have none of them. "These men," writes Mr. Bailey Millard, "admitted the purity of his diction and the magic of his haunting power, but the stories were regarded as revolting."*

At last, in 1891, his first book of stories, Tales of Soldiers and Civilians, *saw the reluctant light of day. It had this for foreword:*

"Denied existence by the chief publishing houses of the country, this book owes itself to Mr. E. L. G. Steele, merchant, of this city,

[San Francisco]. In attesting Mr. Steele's faith in his judgment and his friend, it will serve its author's main and best ambition."

There is Biercean pugnacity in these words; the author flings down the gauntlet with a confident gesture. But it cannot be said that anything much happened to discomfit the publishing houses of little faith. Apparently, Bierce had thought to appeal past the dull and unjust verdict of such lower courts to the higher tribunal of the critics and possibly an elect group of general readers who might be expected to recognize and welcome something rare. But judgment was scarcely reversed. Only a few critics were discerning, and the book had no vogue. When The Monk and the Hangman's Daughter *was published by F. J. Schulte and Company, Chicago, the next year, and* Can Such Things Be *by The Cassell Publishing Company, the year following, a few enthusiastic critics could find no words strong enough to describe Bierce's vivid imagination, his uncanny divination of atavistic terrors in man's consciousness, his chiseled perfection of style; but the critics who disapproved had even more trouble in finding words strong enough for their purposes and, as before, there was no general appreciation.*

For the next twenty years Ambrose Bierce was a prolific writer but, whatever the reason, no further volumes of stories from his pen were presented to the world. Black Beetles in Amber, *a collection of satiric verse, had appeared the same year as* The Monk and the Hangman's Daughter; *then for seven years, with the exception of a republication by G. P. Putnam's Sons of* Tales of Soldiers and Civilians *under the title,* In the Midst of Life, *no books by Bierce. In 1899 appeared* Fantastic Fables; *in 1903* Shapes of Clay, *more satiric verse; in 1906* The Cynic's Word Book, *a dictionary of wicked epigrams; in 1909* Write it Right, *a blacklist of literary faults, and* The Shadow on the Dial, *a collection of essays covering, to quote from the preface of S. O. Howes, "a wide range of subjects, embracing among other things, government, dreams, writers of dialect and dogs"—Mr. Howes might have heightened his crescendo by adding "emancipated woman"; and finally—1909 to 1912—*The Collected Works of Ambrose Bierce, *containing all his work previously published in book form, save the two last mentioned, and much more besides, all collected and edited by Bierce himself.*

On October 2, 1913, Ambrose Bierce, having settled his business affairs, left Washington for a trip through the southern states, declaring in letters his purpose of going into Mexico and later on to South America. The fullest account of his trip and his plans is afforded by a newspaper clipping he sent his niece in a letter dated November 6, 1913; through the commonplaceness of the reportorial vocabulary shines out the vivid personality that was making its final exit:

"Traveling over the same ground that he had covered with General Hazen's brigade during the Civil War, Ambrose Bierce, famed writer and noted critic, has arrived in New Orleans. Not that this city was one of the places figuring in his campaigns, for he was here after and not during the war. He has come to New Orleans in a haphazard, fancy-free way, making a trip toward

Mexico. The places that he has visited on the way down have become famous in song and story—places where the greatest battles were fought, where the moon shone at night on the burial corps, and where in day the sun shone bright on polished bayonets and the smoke drifted upward from the cannon mouths.

"For Mr. Bierce was at Chickamauga; he was at Shiloh; at Murfreesboro; Kenesaw Mountain, Franklin and Nashville. And then when wounded during the Atlanta campaign he was invalided home. He 'has never amounted to much since then,' he said Saturday. But his stories of the great struggle, living as deathless characterizations of the bloody episodes, stand for what he 'has amounted to since then.'

"Perhaps it was in mourning for the dead over whose battle-fields he has been wending his way toward New Orleans that Mr. Bierce was dressed in black. From head to foot he was attired in this color, except where the white cuffs and collar and shirt front showed through. He even carried a walking cane, black as ebony and unrelieved by gold or silver. But his eyes, blue and piercing as when they strove to see through the smoke at Chickamauga, retained all the fire of the indomitable fighter.

"'I'm on my way to Mexico, because I like the game,' he said, 'I like the fighting; I want to see it. And then I don't think Americans are as oppressed there as they say they are, and I want to get at the true facts of the case. Of course, I'm not going into the country if I find it unsafe for Americans to be there, but I want to take a trip diagonally across from northeast to southwest by horseback, and then take ship for South America, go over the Andes and across that continent, if possible, and come back to America again.

"'There is no family that I have to take care of; I've retired from writing and I'm going to take a rest. No, my trip isn't for

*local color. I've retired just the same as a merchant or business
man retires. I'm leaving the field for the younger authors.'*

*"An inquisitive question was interjected as to whether Mr.
Bierce had acquired a competency only from his writings, but he
did not take offense.*

*"'My wants are few, and modest,' he said, 'and my royalties
give me quite enough to live on. There isn't much that I need,
and I spend my time in quiet travel. For the last five years I
haven't done any writing. Don't you think that after a man has
worked as long as I have that he deserves a rest? But perhaps
after I have rested I might work some more—I can't tell, there
are so many things—' and the straightforward blue eyes took on
a faraway look, 'there are so many things that might happen between now and when I come back. My trip might take several
years, and I'm an old man now.'*

*"Except for the thick, snow-white hair no one would think him
old. His hands are steady, and he stands up straight and tall—
perhaps six feet."*

*In December of that same year the last letter he is known
to have written was received by his daughter. It is dated
from Chihuahua, and mentions casually that he has attached himself unofficially to a division of Villa's army, and
speaks of a prospective advance on Ojinaga. No further
word has ever come from or of Ambrose Bierce. Whether
illness overtook him, then an old man of seventy-one, and
death suddenly, or whether, preferring to go foaming over
a precipice rather than to straggle out in sandy deltas, he
deliberately went where he knew death was, no one can say.
His last letters, dauntless, grave, tender, do not say, though
they suggest much. "You must try to forgive my obstinacy*

in not 'perishing' where I am," he wrote as he left Washington. "I want to be where something worth while is going
on, or where nothing whatever is going on." "Good-bye—
if you hear of my being stood up against a Mexican stone
wall and shot to rags please know that I think that a pretty
good way to depart this life. It beats old age, disease, or falling down the cellar stairs. To be a Gringo in Mexico—ah,
that is euthanasia!" Whatever end Ambrose Bierce found
in Mexico, the lines of George Sterling well express what
must have been his attitude in meeting it:

> "Dream you he was afraid to live?
> Dream you he was afraid to die?
> Or that, a suppliant of the sky,
> He begged the gods to keep or give?
> Not thus the shadow-maker stood,
>   Whose scrutiny dissolved so well
>   Our thin mirage of Heven or Hell—
> The doubtful evil, dubious good. . . .
>
> "If now his name be with the dead,
>   And where the gaunt agaves flow'r,
>   The vulture and the wolf devour
> The lion-heart, the lion-head,
> Be sure that heart and head were laid
>   In wisdom down, content to die;
>   Be sure he faced the Starless Sky
> Unduped, unmurmuring, unafraid."

In any consideration of the work of Ambrose Bierce, a central question must be why it contains so much that is trivial
or ephemeral. Another question facing every critic of Bierce,

is why the fundamentally original point of view, the clarity of workmanship of his best things—mainly stories—did not win him immediate and general recognition.

A partial answer to both questions is to be found in a certain discord between Bierce and his setting. Bierce, paradoxically, combined the bizarre in substance, the severely restrained and compressed in form. An ironic mask covered a deep-seated sensibility; but sensibility and irony were alike subject to an uncompromising truthfulness; he would have given deep-throated acclaim to Clough's

> " But play no tricks upon thy soul, O man,
>   Let truth be truth, and life the thing it can."

He had the aristocrat's contempt for mass feeling, a selectiveness carried so far that he instinctively chose for themes the picked person and experience, the one decisive moment of crisis. He viewed his characters not in relation to other men and in normal activities; he isolated them—often amid abnormalities.

All this was in sharp contrast to the literary fashion obtaining when he dipped his pen to try his luck as a creative artist. The most popular novelist of the day was Dickens; the most popular poet, Tennyson. Neither looked straight at life; both veiled it: one in benevolence, the other in beauty. Direct and painful verities were best tolerated by the reading public when exhibited as instances of the workings of natural law. The spectator of the macrocosm in action could stomach the wanton destruction of a given human atom; one so privileged could and did excuse the Creator for small mis-

takes like harrying Hetty Sorrell to the gallow's foot, because of the conviction that, taking the Universe by and
large, "He was a good fellow, and 'twould all be well."
This benevolent optimism was the offspring of a strange
pair, evangelicism and evolution; and in the minds of the
great public whom Bierce, under other circumstances and
with a slightly different mixture of qualities in himself,
might have conquered, it became a large, soft insincerity
that demanded "happy endings," a profuse broadness of
treatment prohibitive of harsh simplicity, a swathing of
elemental emotion in gentility or moral edification.

But to Bierce's mind, "noble and nude and antique," this
mid-Victorian draping and bedecking of "unpleasant
truths" was abhorrent. Absolutely direct and unafraid—
not only in his personal relations but, what is more rare, in
his thinking—he regarded easy optimism, sure that God is
in his heaven with consequently good effects upon the world,
as blindness, and the hopefulness that demanded always
the "happy ending," as silly. In many significant passages
Bierce's attitude is the ironic one of Voltaire: "'Had not
Pangloss got himself hanged,' replied Candide, 'he would
have given us most excellent advice in this emergency; for
he was a profound philosopher.'" Bierce did not fear to bring
in disconcerting evidence that a priori reasoning may prove
a not infallible guide, that causes do not always produce the
effects complacently pre-argued, and that the notion of this
as the best of all possible worlds is sometimes beside the point.

The themes permitted by such an attitude were certain to

displease the readers of that period. In Tales of Soldiers and Civilians, *his first book of stories, he looks squarely and grimly at one much bedecked subject of the time—war; not the fine gay gallantry of war, the music and the marching and the romantic episodes, but the ghastly horror of it; through his vivid, dramatic passages beats a hatred of war, not merely "unrighteous" war, but all war, the more disquieting because never allowed to become articulate. With bitter but beautiful truth he brings each tale to its tragic close, always with one last turn of the screw, one unexpected horror more. And in this book—note the solemn implication of the title he later gave it,* In the Midst of Life—*as well as in the next,* Can Such Things Be, *is still another subject which Bierce alone in his generation seemed unafraid to consider curiously: "Death, in warfare and in the horrid guise of the supernatural, was painted over and over. Man's terror in the face of death gave the artist his cue for his wonderful physical and psychologic microscopics. You could not pin this work down as realism, or as romance; it was the greatest human drama—the conflict between life and death—fused through genius. Not Zola, in the endless pages of his* Debâcle, *not the great Tolstoi in his great* War and Peace *had ever painted war, horrid war, more faithfully than any of the stories of this book; not Maupassant had invented out of war's terrible truths more dramatically imagined plots. . . . There painted an artist who had seen the thing itself, and being a genius, had made it an art still greater.*

Death of the young, the beautiful, the brave, was the clos-

ing note of every line of the ten stories of war in this book. The brilliant, spectacular death that came to such senseless bravery as Tennyson hymned for the music-hall intelligence in his Charge of the Light Brigade; *the vision-starting, slow, soul-drugging death by hanging; the multiplied, comprehensible death that makes rivers near battlefields run red; the death that comes by sheer terror; death actual and imagined—every sort of death was on these pages, so painted as to make Pierre Loti's* Book of Pity and Death *seem but feeble fumbling."*

Now death by the mid-Victorian was considered almost as undesirable an element in society as sex itself. Both must be passed over in silence or presented decently draped. In the eighties any writer who dealt unabashed with death was regarded as an unpleasant person. "Revolting!" cried the critics when they read Bierce's Chickamauga *and* The Affair at Coulter's Notch.

Bierce's style, too, by its very fineness, alienated his public. Superior, keen, perfect in detail, finite, compressed—such was his manner in the free and easy, prolix, rambling, multitudinous nineteenth century.

Bierce himself knew that although it is always the fashion to jeer at fashion, its rule is absolute for all that, whether it be fashion in boots or books.

"A correspondent of mine," he wrote in 1887 in his EXAMINER *column, "a well-known and clever writer, appears surprised because I do not like the work of Robert Louis Stevenson. I am equally hurt to know that he does. If he was*

ever a boy he knows that the year is divided, not into seasons and months, as is vulgarly supposed, but into 'top time,' 'marble time,' 'kite time,' et cetera, and woe to the boy who ignores the unwritten calendar, amusing himself according to the dictates of an irresponsible conscience. I venture to remind my correspondent that a somewhat similar system obtains in matters of literature—a word which I beg him to observe means fiction. There are, for illustration—or rather, there were—James time, Howells time, Crawford time, Russell time and Conway time, each epoch—named for the immortal novelist of the time being—lasting, generally speaking, as much as a year. . . . All the more rigorous is the law of observance. It is not permitted to admire Jones in Smith time. I must point out to my heedless correspondent that this is not Stevenson time—that was last year." It was decidedly not Bierce time when Bierce's stories appeared.

And there was in him no compromise—or so he thought. "A great artist," he wrote to George Sterling, "is superior to his world and his time, or at least to his parish and his day." His practical application of that belief is shown in a letter to a magazine editor who had just rejected a satire he had submitted:

"Even you ask for literature—if my stories are literature, as you are good enough to imply. (By the way, all the leading publishers of the country turned down that book until they saw it published without them by a merchant in San Francisco and another sort of publishers in London, Leipsic and Paris.) Well, you wouldn't do a thing to one of my stories!

"*No, thank you; if I have to write rot, I prefer to do it for the newspapers, which make no false pretenses and are frankly rotten, and in which the badness of a bad thing escapes detection or is forgotten as soon as it is cold.*

"*I know how to write a story (of 'happy ending' sort) for magazine readers for whom literature is too good, but I will not do so, so long as stealing is more honorable and interesting. I have offered you . . . . the best that I am able to make; and now you must excuse me.*" *In these two utterances we have some clue to the secret of his having ceased, in 1893, to publish stories. Vigorously refusing to yield in the slightest degree to the public so far as his stories were concerned, he abandoned his best field of creative effort and became almost exclusively a "columnist" and a satirist; he put his world to rout, and left his "parish and his day" resplendently the victors.*

All this must not be taken to mean that the "form and pressure of the time" put into Bierce what was not there. Even in his creative work he had a satiric bent; his early training and associations, too, had been in journalistic satire. Under any circumstances he undoubtedly would have written satire—columns of it for his daily bread, books of it for self-expression; but under more favorable circumstances he would have kept on writing other sort of books as well. Lovers of literature may well lament that Bierce's insistence on going his way and the demands of his "parish" forced him to overdevelop one power to the almost complete paralysis of another and a perhaps finer.

xxiv   The Introduction

As a satirist Bierce was the best America has produced, perhaps the best since Voltaire. But when he confined himself to "exploring the ways of hate as a form of creative energy," it was with a hurt in his soul, and with some intellectual and spiritual confusion. There resulted a kink in his nature, a contradiction that appears repeatedly, not only in his life, but in his writings. A striking instance is found in his article To Train a Writer:

"*He should, for example, forget that he is an American and remember that he is a man. He should be neither Christian nor Jew, nor Buddhist, nor Mahometan, nor Snake Worshiper. To local standards of right and wrong he should be civilly indifferent. In the virtues, so-called, he should discern only the rough notes of a general expediency; in fixed moral principles only time-saving predecisions of cases not yet before the court of conscience. Happiness should disclose itself to his enlarging intelligence as the end and purpose of life; art and love as the only means to happiness. He should free himself of all doctrines, theories, etiquettes, politics, simplifying his life and mind, attaining clarity with breadth and unity with height. To him a continent should not seem wide nor a century long. And it would be needful that he know and have an ever-present consciousness that this is a world of fools and rogues, blind with superstition, tormented with envy, consumed with vanity, selfish, false, cruel, cursed with illusions—frothing mad!*"

Up to that last sentence Ambrose Bierce beholds this world as one where tolerance, breadth of view, simplicity of life and mind, clear thinking, are at most attainable, at least worthy of the effort to attain; he regards life as purposive, as having happiness for its end, and art and love as the means to that good end. But suddenly the string from which he has been evoking these broad harmonies snaps with a snarl. All is evil and hopeless—"frothing mad." Both views cannot be held simultaneously by the same mind. Which was the real belief of Ambrose Bierce? The former, it seems clear. But he has been hired to be a satirist.

On the original fabric of Bierce's mind the satiric strand has encroached more than the design allows. There results not only considerable obliteration of the main design, but confusion in the substituted one. For it is significant that much of the work of Bierce seems to be that of what he would have called a futilitarian, that he seldoms seems able to find a suitable field for his satire, a foeman worthy of such perfect steel as he brings to the encounter; he fights on all fields, on both sides, against all comers; ubiquitous, indiscriminate, he is as one who screams in pain at his own futility, one who " might be heard," as he says of our civilization, "from afar in space as a scolding and a riot." That Bierce would have spent so much of his superb power on the trivial and the ephemeral, breaking magnificent vials of wrath on Oakland nobodies, preserving insignificant black beetles in the amber of his art, is not merely, as it has long been, cause of amazement to the critics; it is cause of laughter to the gods, and of weeping among Bierce's true admirers.

Some may argue that Bierce's failure to attain international or even national fame cannot be ascribed solely to a lack of concord between the man and his time and to the consequent reaction in him. It is true that in Bierce's work is a sort of paucity—not a mere lack of printed pages, but of the fulness of creative activity that makes Byron, for example, though vulgar and casual, a literary mountain peak. Bierce has but few themes, few moods; his literary river runs clear and sparkling, but confined—a narrow current, not the opulent stream that waters wide plains of thought and feeling. Nor has Bierce the power to weave individual entities and situations into a broad pattern of existence, which is the distinguishing mark of such writers as Thackeray, Balzac, and Tolstoi among the great dead, and Bennett and Wells among the lesser living. Bierce's interest does not lie in the group experience nor even in the experience of the individual through a long period. His unit of time is the minute, not the month. It is significant that he never wrote a novel—unless The Monk and the Hangman's Daughter be reckoned one—and that he held remarkable views of the novel as a literary form, witness this passage from Prattle, written in 1887:

"English novelists are not great because the English novel is dead—deader than Queen Anne at her deadest. The vein is worked out. It was a thin one and did not 'go down.' A single century from the time when Richardson sank the discovery shaft it had already begun to 'pinch out.' The miners of today have abandoned it altogether to search for 'pockets,' and some of the best of them are merely 'chloriding the dumps.' To expect another good novel in English is to expect the gold to 'grow' again."

It may well be that at the bottom of this sweeping condemnation was an instinctive recognition of his own lack of constructive power on a large scale.

But an artist, like a nation, should be judged not by what he cannot do, but by what he can. That Bierce could not paint the large canvas does not make him negligible or even inconsiderable. He is by no means a second-rate writer; he is a first-rate writer who could not consistently show his first-rateness.

When he did show his first-rateness, what is it? In all his best work there is originality, a rare and precious idiosyncracy; his point of view, his themes are rich with it. Above all writers Bierce can present—brilliantly present—startling fragments of life, carved out from attendant circumstance; isolated problems of character and action; sharply bitten etchings of individual men under momentary stresses and in bizarre situations. Through his prodigious emotional perceptivity he has the power of feeling and making us feel some strange, perverse accident of fate, destructive of the individual—of making us feel it to be real and terrible. This is not an easy thing to do. De Maupassant said that men were killed every year in Paris by the falling of tiles from the roof, but if he got rid of a principal character in that way, he should be hooted at. Bierce can make us accept as valid and tragic events more odd than the one de Maupassant had to reject. "In the line of the startling,—half Poe, half Merimee—he cannot have many superiors," says Arnold Bennett. . . . . . "A story like An Occurrence at Owl Creek Bridge—*well, Edgar Allan Poe might have deigned to sign it. And that is something.*

"He possesses a remarkable style—what Kipling's would

have been had Kipling been born with any significance of the word 'art' —and a quite strangely remarkable perception of beauty. There is a feeling for landscape in A Horseman in the Sky *which recalls the exquisite opening of that indifferent novel,* Les Frères Zemganno *by Edmond de Goncourt, and which no English novelist except Thomas Hardy, and possibly Charles Marriott, could match." The feeling for landscape which Bennett notes is but one part of a greater power—the power to make concrete and visible, action, person, place. Bierce's descriptions of Civil War battles in his* Bits of Autobiography *are the best descriptions of battle ever written. He lays out the field with map-like clearness, marshals men and events with precision and economy, but his account never becomes exposition—it is drama. Real battles move swiftly; accounts make them seem labored and slow. What narrator save Bierce can convey the sense of their being lightly swift, and, again and again the shock of surprise the event itself must have given?*

This could not be were it not for his verbal restraint. In his descriptions is no welter of adjectives and adverbs; strong exact nouns and verbs do the work, and this means that the veritable object and action are brought forward, not qualifying talk around and about them. And this, again, could not be were it not for what is, beyond all others, his greatest quality—absolute precision. "I sometimes think," he once wrote playfully about letters of his having been misunderstood, "I sometimes think that I am the only man in the world who understands the meaning of the written word.

Or the only one who does not." A reader of Ambrose Bierce comes almost to believe that not till now has he found a writer who understands—completely—the meaning of the written word. He has the power to bring out new meanings in well-worn words, so setting them as to evoke brilliant significances never before revealed. He gives to one phrase the beauty, the compressed suggestion of a poem; his titles— Black Beetles in Amber, Ashes of the Beacon, Cobwebs from an Empty Skull *are masterpieces in miniature. That he should have a gift of coining striking words naturally follows: in his later years he has fallen into his "anecdotage," a certain Socialist is the greatest "futilitarian" of them all, "femininies,"—and so on infinitely. Often the smaller the Biercean gem, the more exquisite the workmanship. One word has all the sparkle of an epigram.*

In such skill Ambrose Bierce is not surpassed by any writer, ancient or modern; it gives him rank among the few masters who afford that highest form of intellectual delight, the immediate recognition of a clear idea perfectly set forth in fitting words—wit's twin brother, evoking that rare joy, the sudden, secret laughter of the mind. So much for Bierce the artist; the man is found in these letters. If further clue to the real nature of Ambrose Bierce were needed it is to be found in a conversation he had in his later years with a young girl: "You must be very proud, Mr. Bierce, of all your books and your fame?" "No," he answered rather sadly, "you will come to know that all that is worth while in life is the love you have had for a few people near to you."

A Memoir of Ambrose Bierce
by GEORGE STERLING

A Memoir of Ambrose Bierce
by GEORGE STERLING

T HOUGH *from boyhood a lover of tales of the terrible, it was not until my twenty-second year that I heard of Ambrose Bierce, I having then been for ten months a resident of Oakland, California. But in the fall of the year 1891 my friend Roosevelt Johnson, newly arrived from our town of birth, Sag Harbor, New York, asked me if I were acquainted with his work, adding that he had been told that Bierce was the author of stories not inferior in awsomeness to the most terrible of Poe's.*

We made inquiry and found that Bierce had for several years been writing columns of critical comment, satirically named Prattle, *for the editorial page of the Sunday* EXAMINER, *of San Francisco. As my uncle, of whose household I had been for nearly a year a member, did not subscribe to that journal, I had unfortunately overlooked these weekly contributions to the wit and sanity of our western literature—an omission for which we partially consoled ourselves by subsequently reading with great eagerness each installment of* Prattle *as it appeared. But, so far as his short stories were concerned, we had to content ourselves with the assurance of a neighbor that "they'd scare an owl off a tombstone."*

However, later in the autumn, while making a pilgrimage to the home of our greatly worshipped Joaquin Miller, we became acquainted with Albert, an elder brother of Bierce's, a man who was to be one of my dearest of friends to the day of his death, in March, 1914. From him we obtained much to gratify our not unnatural curiosity as to this mysterious being, who, from his isolation on a lonely mountain above the Napa Valley, scattered weekly thunderbolts on the fool, the pretender, and the knave, and cast ridicule or censure on many that sat in the seats of the mighty. For none, however socially or financially powerful, was safe from the stab of that aculeate pen, the venom of whose ink is to gleam vividly from the pages of literature for centuries yet to come.

For Bierce is of the immortals. That fact, known, I think, to him, and seeming then more and more evident to some of his admirers, has become plainly apparent to anyone who can appraise the matter with eyes that see beyond the flimsy artifices that bulk so large and so briefly in the literary arena. Bierce was a sculptor who wrought in hardest crystal.

I was not to be so fortunate as to become acquainted with him until after the publication of his first volume of short stories, entitled Tales of Soldiers and Civilians. *That mild title gives scant indication of the terrors that await the unwarned reader. I recall that I hung fascinated over the book, unable to lay it down until the last of its printed dooms had become an imperishable portion of the memory. The tales are told with a calmness and reserve that make most of Poe's seem somewhat boyish and melodramatic by comparison.*

The greatest of them seems to me to be An Occurrence at Owl Creek Bridge, *though I am perennially charmed by the weird beauty of* An Inhabitant of Carcosa, *a tale of unique and unforgettable quality.*

Bierce, born in Ohio in 1842, came to San Francisco soon after the close of the Civil War. It is amusing to learn that he was one of a family of eleven children, male and female, the Christian name of each of whom began with the letter "A!" Obtaining employment at first in the United States Mint, whither Albert, always his favorite brother, had preceded him, he soon gravitated to journalism, doing his first work on the San Francisco NEWS LETTER. *His brother once told me that he (Ambrose) had from boyhood been eager to become a writer and was expectant of success at that pursuit.*

Isolated from most men by the exalted and austere habit of his thought, Bierce finally suffered a corresponding exile of the body, and was forced to live in high altitudes, which of necessity are lonely. This latter banishment was on account of chronic and utterly incurable asthma, an ailment contracted in what might almost be termed a characteristic manner. Bierce had no fear of the dead folk and their marble city. From occasional strollings by night in Laurel Hill Cemetery, in San Francisco, his spirit "drank repose," and was able to attain a serenity in which the cares of daytime existence faded to nothingness. It was on one of those strolls that he elected to lie for awhile in the moonlight on a flat tombstone, and awakening late in the night, found himself thoroughly chilled, and a subsequent victim of the disease that was to cast so dark a shadow over his following years. For his sufferings from asthma were terrible, arising often to a height that required that he be put under the influence of chloroform.

So afflicted, he found visits to the lowlands a thing not to be indulged in with impunity. For many years such trips terminated invariably in a severe attack of his ailment, and he was driven back to his heights shaken and harassed. But he found such visits both necessary and pleasant on occasion, and it was during one that he made in the summer of 1892 that I first made his acquaintance, while he was temporarily a guest at his brother Albert's camp on a rocky, laurel-covered knoll on the eastern shore of Lake Temescal, a spot now crossed by the tracks of the Oakland, Antioch and Eastern Railway.

I am not likely to forget his first night among us. A tent being, for his ailment, insufficiently ventilated, he decided to sleep by the campfire, and I, carried away by my youthful hero-worship, must partially gratify it by occupying the side of the fire opposite to him. I had a comfortable cot in my tent, and was unaccustomed at the time to sleeping on the ground, the consequence being that I awoke at least every half-hour. But awake as often as I might, always I found Bierce lying on his back in the dim light of the embers, his gaze fixed on the stars of the zenith. I shall not forget the gaze of those eyes, the most piercingly blue, under yellow shaggy brows, that I have ever seen.

After that, I saw him at his brother's home in Berkeley, at irregular intervals, and once paid him a visit at his own temporary home at Skylands, above Wrights, in Santa Clara County, whither he had moved from Howell Mountain, in Napa County. It was on this visit that I was emboldened to ask his opinion on certain verses of mine, the ambition to become a poet having infected me at the scandalously mature age of twenty-six. He was hospitable to my wish, and I was fortunate enough to be his pupil almost to the year of his going forth from among us. During the greater part of that time he was a resident of Washington, D.C., whither he had gone in behalf of the San Francisco EXAMINER, to aid in defeating (as was successfully accomplished) the Funding Bill proposed by the Southern Pacific Company. It was on this occasion that he electrified the Senate's committee by repeatedly refusing to shake the hand of the proponent of that measure, no less formidable an individual than Collis P. Huntington.

For Bierce carried into actual practice his convictions on ethical matters. Secure in his own self-respect, and valuing his friendship or approval to a high degree, he refused to make, as he put it, " a harlot of his friendship." Indeed, he once told me that it was his rule, on subsequently discovering the unworth of a person to whom a less fastidious friend had without previous warning introduced him, to write a letter to that person and assure him that he regarded the introduction as a mistake, and that the twain were thenceforth to "meet as strangers!" He also once informed me that he did not care to be introduced to persons whom he had criticized, or was about to criticize, in print. "I might get to like the beggar," was his comment, "and then I'd have one less pelt in my collection."

In his criticism of my own work, he seldom used more than suggestion, realizing, no doubt, the sensitiveness of the tyro in poetry. It has been hinted to me that he laid, as it were, a hand of ice on my youthful enthusiasms, but that, to such extent as it may be true, was, I think, a good thing for a pupil of the art, youth being apt to gush and become over-sentimental. Most poets would give much to be able to obliterate some of their earlier work, and he must have saved me a major portion of such putative embarrassment. Reviewing the manuscripts that bear his marginal counsels, I can now see that such suggestions were all "indicated," though at the time I dissented from some of them. It was one of his tenets that a critic should "keep his heart out of his head" (to use his own words), when sitting in judgment on the work of writers whom he knew and liked. But I cannot but think that he was guilty of sad violations of that rule, especially in my own case.

Bierce lived many years in Washington before making a visit to his old home. That happened in 1910, in which year he visited me at Carmel, and we afterwards camped for several weeks together with his brother and nephew, in Yosemite. I grew to know him better in those days, and he found us hospitable, in the main degree, to his view of things, socialism being the only issue on which we were not *in accord. It led to many warm arguments, which, as usual, conduced nowhere but to the suspicion that truth in such matters was mainly a question of taste.*

I saw him again in the summer of 1911, which he spent at Sag Harbor. We were much on the water, guests of my uncle in his power-yacht " La Mascotte II." He was a devotee of canoeing, and made many trips on the warm and shallow bays of eastern Long Island, which he seemed to prefer to the less spacious reaches of the Potomac. He revisited California in the fall of the next year, a trip on which we saw him for the last time. An excursion to the Grand Canyon was occasionally proposed, but nothing came of it, nor did he consent to be again my guest at Carmel, on the rather surprising excuse that the village contained too many anarchists! And in November, 1913, I received my last letter from him, he being then in Laredo, Texas, about to cross the border into warring Mexico.

Why he should have gone forth on so hazardous an enterprise is for the most part a matter of conjecture. It may have been in the spirit of adventure, or out of boredom, or he may not, even, have been jesting when he wrote to an intimate friend that, ashamed of having lived so long, and not caring to end his life by his own hand, he was going across the border and let the Mexicans perform for him that service. But he wrote to others that he purposed to extend his pilgrimage as far as South America, to cross the Andes, and return to New York by way of a steamer from Buenos Ayres. At any rate, we know, from letters written during

the winter months, that he had unofficially attached him-
self to a section of Villa's army, even taking an active part
in the fighting. He was heard from until the close of 1913;
after that date the mist closes in upon his trail, and we are
left to surmise what we may. Many rumors as to his fate
have come out of Mexico, one of them even placing him in
the trenches of Flanders. These rumors have been, so far as
possible, investigated: all end in nothing. The only one that
seems in the least degree illuminative is the tale brought by
a veteran reporter from the City of Mexico, and published
in the San Francisco BULLETIN. It is the story of a soldier in
Villa's army, one of a detachment that captured, near the
village of Icamole, an ammunition train of the Carran-
zistas. One of the prisoners was a sturdy, white-haired,
ruddy-faced Gringo, who, according to the tale, went be-
fore the firing squad with an Indian muleteer, as sole com-
panion in misfortune. The description of the manner—in-
different, even contemptuous—with which the white-haired
man met his death seems so characteristic of Bierce that
one would almost be inclined to give credence to the tale,
impossible though it may be of verification. But the date of
the tragedy being given as late in 1915, it seems incredible
that Bierce could have escaped observation for so long a
period, with so many persons in Mexico eager to know of his
fate. It is far more likely that he met his death at the hands
of a roving band of outlaws or guerrilla soldiery.

I have had often in mind the vision of his capture by such
a squad, their discovery of the considerable amount of gold

coin that he was known to carry on his person, and his immediate condemnation and execution as a spy in order that
they might retain possession of the booty. Naturally, such
proceedings would not have been reported, from fear of the
necessity of sharing with those "higher up." And so the veil
would have remained drawn, and impenetrable to vision.
Through the efforts of the War Department, all United
States Consuls were questioned as to Bierce's possible departure from the country; all Americans visiting or resid-
ing in Mexico were begged for information—even pros-
pectors. But the story of the reporter is the sole one that seems
partially credible. To such darkness did so shining and fear-
less a soul go forth.

It is now over eight years since that disappearance, and
though the likelihood of his existence in the flesh seems faint
indeed, the storm of detraction and obloquy that he always
insisted would follow his demise has never broken, is not
even on the horizon. Instead, he seems to be remembered with
tolerance by even those whom he visited with a chastening
pen. Each year of darkness but makes the star of his fame
increase and brighten, but we have, I think, no full conception as yet of his greatness, no adequate realization of
how wide and permanent a fame he has won. It is significant that some of the discerning admire him for one phase
of his work, some for another. For instance, the clear-headed
H. L. Mencken acclaims him as the first wit of America,
but will have none of his tales; while others, somewhat dis-
concerted by the cynicism pervading much of his wit, place

him among the foremost exponents of the art of the short story. Others again prefer his humor (for he was humorist as well as wit), and yet others like most the force, clarity and keen insight of his innumerable essays and briefer comments on mundane affairs. Personally, I have always regarded Poe's Fall of the House of Usher *as our greatest tale; close to that come, in my opinion, at least a dozen of Bierce's stories, whether of the soldier or civilian. He has himself stated in* Prattle: *"I am not a poet." And yet he wrote poetry, on occasion, of a high order, his* Invocation *being one of the noblest poems in the tongue. Some of his satirical verse seems to me as terrible in its withering invective as any that has been written by classic satirists, not excepting Juvenal and Swift. Like the victims of their merciless pens, his, too, will be forgiven and forgotten. Today no one knows, nor cares, whether or not those long-dead offenders gave just offense. The grave has closed over accuser and accused, and the only thing that matters is that a great mind was permitted to function. One may smile or sigh over the satire, but one must also realize that even the satirist had his own weaknesses, and could have been as savagely attacked by a mentality as keen as his own. Men as a whole will never greatly care for satire, each recognizing, true enough, glimpses of himself in the invective, but sensing as well its fundamental bias and cruelty. However, Bierce thought best of himself as a satirist.*

Naturally, Bierce carried his wit and humor into his immediate human relationships. I best recall an occasion, when, in my first year of acquaintance with him, we were both guests at the home of the painter, J. H. E. Partington. It happened that a bowl of nasturtiums adorned the center table, and having been taught by Father Tabb, the poet, to relish that flower, I managed to consume most of them before the close of the evening, knowing there were plenty more to be had in the garden outside. Someone at last remarked: "Why, George has eaten all the nasturtiums! Go out and bring some more." At which Bierce dryly and justly remarked: "No—bring some thistles!" It is an indication, however, of his real kindness of heart that, observing my confusion, he afterwards apologized to me for what he termed a thoughtless jest. It was, nevertheless, well deserved.

I recall even more distinctly a scene of another setting. This concerns itself with Bierce's son, Leigh, then a youth in the early twenties. At the time (circa *1894*) *I was a brother lodger with them in an Oakland apartment house. Young Bierce had contracted a liaison with a girl of his own age, and his father, determined to end the affair, had appointed an hour for discussion of the matter. The youth entered his father's rooms defiant and resolute: within an hour he appeared weeping, and cried out to me, waiting for him in his own room: " My father is a greater man than Christ! He has suffered more than Christ!" And the affair of the heart was promptly terminated.*

One conversant with Bierce only as a controversionalist and censor morum *was, almost of necessity, constrained to imagine him a misanthrope, a soured and cynical recluse.*

Only when one was privileged to see him among his intimates could one obtain glimpses of his true nature, which was considerate, generous, even affectionate. Only the waving of the red flag of Socialism could rouse in him what seemed to us others a certain savageness of intolerance. Needless to say, we did not often invoke it, for he was an ill man with whom to bandy words. It was my hope, at one time, to involve him and Jack London in a controversy on the subject, but London declined the oral encounter, preferring one with the written word. Nothing came of the plan, which is a pity, as each was a supreme exponent of his point of view. Bierce subsequently attended one of the midsummer encampments of the Bohemian Club, of which he was once the secretary, in their redwood grove near the Russian river. Hearing that London was present, he asked why they had not been mutually introduced, and I was forced to tell him that I feared that they'd be, verbally, at each other's throats, within an hour. "Nonsense!" exclaimed Bierce. "Bring him around! I'll treat him like a Dutch Uncle." He kept his word, and seemed as much attracted to London as London was to him. But I was always ill at ease when they were conversing. I do not think the two men ever met again.

Bierce was the cleanest man, personally, of whom I have knowledge—almost fanatically so, if such a thing be possible. Even during our weeks of camping in the Yosemite, he would spend two hours on his morning toilet in the privacy of his tent. His nephew always insisted that the time was devoted to shaving himself from face to foot! He was also a most modest man, and I still recall his decided objections to my bathing attire when at the swimming-pool of the Bohemian Club, in the Russian River. Compared to many of those visible, it seemed more than adequate; but he had another opinion of it. He was a good, even an eminent, tankard-man, and retained a clear judgment under any amount of potations. He preferred wine (especially a dry vin du pays, usually a sauterne) to "hard likker," in this respect differing in taste from his elder brother. In the days when I first made his acquaintance, I was accustomed to roam the hills beyond Oakland and Berkeley from Cordonices Creek to Leona Heights, in company with Albert Bierce, his son Carlton, R.L. ("Dick") Partington, Leigh Bierce (Ambrose's surviving son) and other youths. On such occasions I sometimes hid a superfluous bottle of port or sherry in a convenient spot, and Bierce, afterwards accompanying us on several such outings, pretended to believe that I had such flagons concealed under each bush or rock in the reach and breadth of the hills, and would, to carry out the jest, hunt zealously in such recesses. I could wish that he were less often unsuccessful in the search, now that he has had "the coal-black wine" to drink.

Though an appreciable portion of his satire hints at misanthropy, Bierce, while profoundly a pessimist, was, by his own confession to me, "a lover of his country and his fellowmen," and was ever ready to proffer assistance in the time of need and sympathy in the hour of sorrow. His was a great and tender heart, and giving of it greatly, he expected, or *rather hoped for, a return as great. It may have been by reason of the frustration of such hopes that he so often broke with old and, despite his doubts, appreciative friends. His brother Albert once told me that he (Ambrose) had never been "quite the same," after the wound in the head that he received in the battle of Kenesaw Mountain, but had a tendency to become easily offended and to show that resentment. Such estrangements as he and his friends suffered are not, therefore, matters on which one should sit in judgment. It is sad to know that he went so gladly from life, grieved and disappointed. But the white flame of Art that he tended for nearly half a century was never permitted to grow faint nor smoky, and it burned to the last with a pure brilliance. Perhaps, he bore witness to what he had found most admirable and enduring in life in the following words, the conclusion of the finest of his essays:*

" Literature and art are about all that the world really cares for in the end; those who make them are not without justification in regarding themselves as masters in the House of Life and all others as their servitors. In the babble and clamor, the pranks and antics of its countless incapables, the tremendous dignity of the profession of letters is overlooked; but when, casting a retrospective eye into 'the dark backward and abysm of time' to where beyond these voices is the peace of desolation, we note the majesty of the few immortals and compare them with the pygmy figures of their contemporary kings, warriors and men of action generally— when across the silent battle-fields and hushed fora *where*

the dull destinies of nations were determined, nobody cares how, we hear

> *like ocean on a western beach*
> *The surge and thunder of the Odyssey,*

then we appraise literature at its true value, and how little worth while seems all else with which Man is pleased to occupy his fussy soul and futile hands!''

The Letters of Ambrose Bierce

The Letters of Ambrose Bierce

My dear Blanche,

You will not, I hope, mind my saying that the first part of your letter was so pleasing that it almost solved the disappointment created by the other part. For *that* is a bit discouraging. Let me explain.

You receive my suggestion about trying your hand * * * at writing, with assent and apparently pleasure. But, alas, not for love of the art, but for the purpose of helping God repair his botchwork world. You want to "reform things," poor girl — to rise and lay about you, slaying monsters and liberating captive maids. You would "help to alter for the better the position of working-women." You would be a missionary — and the rest of it. Perhaps I shall not make myself understood when I say that this discourages me; that in such aims (worthy as they are) I would do nothing to assist you; that such ambitions are not only impracticable but incompatible with the spirit that gives success in art; that such ends are a prostitution of art; that "helpful" writing is dull reading. If you had had more experience of life I should regard what you say as entirely conclusive against your possession of any talent of a literary kind. But you are so young and untaught in that way — and I have the testimony of little felicities and purely literary touches (apparently unconscious) in your letters — perhaps your

Angwin,
July 31,
1892.

unschooled heart and hope should not be held as having spoken the conclusive word. But surely, my child — as surely as anything in mathematics — Art will laurel no brow having a divided allegiance. Love the world as much as you will, but serve it otherwise. The best service you can perform by writing is to write well with no care for anything but that. Plant and water and let God give the increase if he will, and to whom it shall please him.

Suppose your father were to "help working-women" by painting no pictures but such (of their ugly surroundings, say) as would incite them to help themselves, or others to help them. Suppose you should play no music but such as — but I need go no further. Literature (I don't mean journalism) is an *art;* — it is not a form of benevolence. It has nothing to do with "reform," and when used as a means of reform suffers accordingly and justly. Unless you can *feel* that way I cannot advise you to meddle with it.

It would be dishonest in me to accept your praise for what I wrote of the Homestead Works quarrel — unless you should praise it for being well written and true. I have no sympathies with that savage fight between the two kinds of rascals, and no desire to assist either — except to better hearts and manners. The love of truth is good enough motive for me when I write of my fellowmen. I like many things in this world and a few persons — I like you, for example; but after they are served I have no love to waste upon the irreclaimable mass of brutality that we know as "mankind." Compassion, yes — I am sincerely sorry that they are brutes.

Yes, I wrote the article "The Human Liver." Your criticism is erroneous. My opportunities of knowing women's feelings toward Mrs. Grundy are better than yours. They hate her with a horrible antipathy; but they cower all the same. The fact that they are a part of her mitigates neither their hatred nor their fear.

* * *

After next Monday I shall probably be in St. Helena, but if you will be so good as still to write to me please address me here until I apprise you of my removal; for I shall intercept my letters at St. Helena, wherever addressed. And maybe you will write before Monday. I need not say how pleasant it is for me to hear from you. And I shall want to know what you think of what I say about your "spirit of reform."

How I should have liked to pass that Sunday in camp with you all. And to-day—I wonder if you are there to-day. I feel a peculiar affection for that place.

Please give my love to all your people, and forgive my intolerably long letters — or retaliate in kind.

Sincerely your friend,
AMBROSE BIERCE.

I KNOW, DEAR BLANCHE, of the disagreement among men as to the nature and aims of literature; and the subject is too "long" to discuss. I will only say that it seems to me that men holding Tolstoi's view are not properly literary men (that is to say, artists) at all. They are "missionaries," who, in their zeal to lay about them, do not scruple to seize any weapon that they can lay their hands on; they would grab a crucifix to beat a dog. The dog is well beaten, no doubt (which makes him a worse dog than he was before) but note the condition of the crucifix! The work of these men is better, of course, than the work of men of truer art and inferior brains; but always you see the possi-

St. Helena, August 15, 1892.

bilities — possibilities to *them* — which they have missed or consciously sacrificed to their fad. And after all they do no good. The world does not wish to be helped. The poor wish only to be rich, which is impossible, not to be better. They would like to be rich in order to be worse, generally speaking. And your working woman (also generally speaking) does not wish to be virtuous; despite her insincere deprecation she would not let the existing system be altered if she could help it. Individual men and women can be assisted; and happily some are worthy of assistance. No *class* of mankind, no tribe, no nation is worth the sacrifice of one good man or woman; for not only is their average worth low, but they like it that way; and in trying to help them you fail to help the good individuals. Your family, your immediate friends, will give you scope enough for all your benevolence. I must include your*self*.

In timely illustration of some of this is an article by Ingersoll in the current *North American Review* —I shall send it you. It will be nothing new to you; the fate of the philanthropist who gives out of his brain and heart instead of his pocket — having nothing in that — is already known to you. It serves him richly right, too, for his low taste in loving. He who dilutes, spreads, subdivides, the love which naturally *all* belongs to his family and friends (if they are good) should not complain of non-appreciation. Love those, help those, whom from personal knowledge you know to be worthy. To love and help others is treason to *them*. But, bless my soul! I did not mean to say all this.

But while you seem clear as to your own art, you seem undecided as to the one you wish to take up. I know the strength and sweetness of the illusions (that is, *de*lusions) that you are required to forego. I know the abysmal ignorance of the world and human character which, as a girl, you necessarily have. I know the charm that inheres in the beckoning of the Britomarts, as they lean out of their dream to persuade you to be as like them as is compatible with the fact that you exist. But I believe, too, that if you are set thinking — not reading — you will find the light.

You ask me of journalism. It is so low a thing that it *may* be legitimately used as a means of reform or a means of anything deemed worth accomplishing. It is not an art; art, except in the greatest moderation, is damaging to it. The man who can write well must not write as well as he can; the others may, of course. Journalism has many purposes, and the people's welfare *may* be one of them; though that is not the purpose-in-chief, by much.

I don't mind your irony about my looking upon the unfortunate as merely "literary material." It is true in so far as I consider them *with reference to literature*. Possibly I might be willing to help them otherwise — as your father might be willing to help a beggar with money, who is not picturesque enough to go into a picture. As you might be willing to give a tramp a dinner, yet unwilling to play "The Sweet Bye-and-Bye," or "Ta-ra-ra-boom-de-ay," to tickle his ear.

You call me "master." Well, it is pleasant to think of you as a pupil, but — you know the young squire had to watch his arms all night before the day of his accolade and investiture with knighthood. I think I'll ask you to contemplate yours a little longer before donning them — not by way of penance but instruction and consecration. When you are quite sure of the nature of your *call* to write — quite sure that it is *not* the voice of "duty" — then let me do you such slight, poor service as my limitations and the injunctions of circumstance permit. In a few ways I can help you.   * * *

Since coming here I have been ill all the time, but it seems my duty to remain as long as there is a hope that I *can* remain. If I get free from my disorder and the fear of it I shall go down to San Francisco some day and then try to see your people and mine. Perhaps you would help me to find my brother's new house — if he is living in it.

With sincere regards to all your family, I am most truly your friend,   AMBROSE BIERCE.

Your letters are very pleasing to me. I think it nice of you to write them.   ❧ ❧ ❧

St. Helena,   DEAR BLANCHE,
August 17,
1892.   It was not that I forgot to mail you the magazine that I mentioned; I could not find it; but now I send it.

My health is bad again, and I fear that I shall have to abandon my experiment of living here, and go back to the mountain — or some mountain. But not directly.

You asked me what books would be useful to you — I'm assuming that you've repented your sacrilegious attitude toward literature, and will endeavor to thrust your pretty head into the crown of martyrdom otherwise. I may mention a few from time to time as they occur to me. There is a little book entitled (I think) simply "English Composition." It is by Prof. John Nichol — elementary, in a few places erroneous, but on the whole rather better than the ruck of books on the same subject.

Read those of Landor's "Imaginary Conversations" which relate to literature.

Read Longinus, Herbert Spencer on Style, Pope's "Essay on Criticism" (don't groan—the detractors of Pope are not always to have things their own way), Lucian on the writing of history — though you need not write history. Read poor old obsolete Kames' notions; some of them are not half bad. Read Burke "On the Sublime and Beautiful."

Read—but that will do at present. And as you read don't forget that the rules of the literary art are deduced from the work of the masters who wrote in ignorance of them or in unconsciousness of them. That fixes their value; it is secondary to that of *natural* qualifications. None the less, it is considerable. Doubtless you have read many — perhaps most — of these things, but to read them with a view to profit *as a writer* may be different. If I could get to San Francisco I could dig out of those artificial memories, the catalogues of the libraries, a lot of titles additional — and get you the books, too. But I've a bad memory, and am out of the Book Belt.

I wish you would write some little thing and send it me for examination. I shall not judge it harshly, for this I *know:* the good writer (supposing him to be born to the trade) is not made by reading, but by observing and experiencing. You have lived so little, seen so little, that your range will necessarily be narrow, but within its lines I know no reason why you should not do good work. But it is all conjectural — you may fail. Would it hurt if I should tell you that I thought you had failed? Your absolute and complete failure would not affect in the slightest my admiration of your intellect. I have always half suspected that it is only second rate minds, and minds below the second rate, that hold their cleverness by so precarious a tenure that they can detach it for display in words.

God bless you,

A. B.

St. Helena,
August 28,
1892.

My dear Blanche,

I positively shall not bore you with an interminated screed this time. But I thought you might like to know that I have recovered my health, and hope to be able to remain here for a few months at least. And if I remain well long enough to make me reckless I shall visit your town some day, and maybe ask your mother to command you to let me drive you to Berkeley. It makes me almost sad to think of the camp at the lake being abandoned.

So you liked my remarks on the "labor question." That is nice of you, but aren't you afraid your praise will get me into the disastrous literary habit of writing for some *one* pair of eyes? — your eyes? Or in resisting the temptation I may go too far in the opposite error. But you do not see that it is "Art for Art's sake" — hateful phrase! Certainly not, it is not Art at all. Do you forget the distinction I pointed out between journalism and literature? Do you not remember that I told you that the former was of so little value that it might be used for anything? My newspaper work is in *no* sense literature. It is nothing, and only becomes something when I give it the very use to which I would put nothing literary. (Of course I refer to my editorial and topical work.)

If you want to learn to write that kind of thing, so as to do good with it, you've an easy task. *Only* it is not worth learning and the good that you can do with it is not worth doing. But literature — the desire to do good with *that* will not help you to your means. It is not a sufficient incentive. The Muse will not meet you if you have any work for her to do. Of course I sometimes like to do good — who does not? And sometimes I am glad that access to a great number of minds every week gives me an opportunity. But, thank Heaven, I don't make a business of it, nor use in it a tool so delicate as to be ruined by the service.

Please do not hesitate to send me anything that you may be willing to write. If you try to make it perfect before you let me see it, it will never come. My remarks about the kind of mind which holds its thoughts and feelings by so precarious a tenure that they are detachable for use by others were not made with a forethought of your failure.

Mr. Harte of the New England Magazine seems to want me to know his work (I asked to) and sends me a lot of it cut from the magazine. I pass it on to you, and most of it is just and true.

But I'm making another long letter.

I wish I were not an infidel — so that I could say: "God bless you," and mean it literally. I wish there *were* a God to bless you, and that He had nothing else to do.

Please let me hear from you. Sincerely,   A. B.

My dear Blanche,

I have been waiting for a full hour of leisure to write you a letter, but I shall never get it, and so I'll write you anyhow. Come to think of it, there is nothing to say — nothing that *needs* be said, rather, for there is always so much that one would like to say to you, best and most patient of *sayees*.

St. Helena, September 28, 1892.

I'm sending you and your father copies of my book. Not that I think you (either of you) will care for that sort of thing, but merely because your father is my co-sinner in making the book, and you in sitting by and diverting my mind from the proof-sheets of a part of it. Your part, therefore, in the work is the typographical errors. So you are in literature in spite of yourself.

I appreciate what you write of my girl. She is the best of girls to me, but God knoweth I'm not a proper person to direct her way of life. However, it will not be for long. A dear friend of mine — the widow of another dear friend — in London wants her, and means to come out here next spring and try to persuade me to let her have her — for a time at least. It is likely that I shall. My friend is wealthy, childless and devoted to both my children. I wish that in the meantime she (the girl) could have the advantage of association with *you*.

Please say to your father that I have his verses, which I promise myself pleasure in reading.

You appear to have given up your ambition to "write things." I'm sorry, for "lots" of reasons — not the least being the selfish one that I fear I shall be deprived of a reason for writing you long dull letters. Won't you *play* at writing things?

My (and Danziger's) book, "The Monk and the Hangman's Daughter," is to be out next month. The Publisher — I like to write it with a reverent capital letter — is unprofessional enough to tell me that he regards it as the very best piece of English composition that he ever saw, and he means to make the world know it. Now let the great English classics hide their diminished heads and pale their ineffectual fires!

So you begin to suspect that books do not give you the truth of life and character. Well, that suspicion is the beginning of wisdom, and, so far as it goes, a preliminary qualification for writing — books. Men and women are certainly not what books represent them to be, nor what *they* represent — and sometimes believe — themselves to be. They are better, they are worse, and far more interesting.

With best regards to all your people, and in the hope that we may frequently hear from you, I am very sincerely your friend,   AMBROSE BIERCE.

Both the children send their *love* to you. And they mean just that.

MY DEAR BLANCHE,

I send you by this mail the current *New England Maga-* St. Helena,
zine — merely because I have it by me and have read all October 6,
of it that I shall have leisure to read. Maybe it will enter- 1892.
tain you for an idle hour.

I have so far recovered my health that I hope to do a little pot-boiling to-morrow. (Is that properly written with a hyphen? — for the life o' me I can't say, just at this moment. There is a story of an old actor who having played one part half his life had to cut out the name of the person he represented wherever it occurred in his lines: he could never remember which syllable to accent.) My ill-ness was only asthma, which, unluckily, does not kill me and so should not alarm my friends.

Dr. Danziger writes that he has ordered your father's sketch sent me. And I've ordered a large number of extra impres-sions of it — if it is still on the stone. So you see I like it.

Let me hear from you and about you.

Sincerely your friend,
I enclose Bib.   AMBROSE BIERCE.

DEAR MR. PARTINGTON,

I've been too ill all the week to write you of your manu- St. Helena,
scripts, or even read them understandingly.   October 7,
                                                            1892.
I think "Honest Andrew's Prayer" far and away the best. *It* is witty — the others hardly more than earnest, and not, in my judgment, altogether fair. But then you

know you and I would hardly be likely to agree on a point of that kind, — I refuse my sympathies in some directions where I extend my sympathy — if that is intelligible. You, I think, have broader sympathies than mine — are not only sorry for the Homestead strikers (for example) but approve them. I do not. But we are one in detesting their oppressor, the smug-wump, Carnegie.

If you had not sent "Honest Andrew's Prayer" elsewhere I should try to place it here. It is so good that I hope to see it in print. If it is rejected please let me have it again if the incident is not then ancient history.

I'm glad you like some things in my book. But you should not condemn me for debasing my poetry with abuse; you should commend me for elevating my abuse with a little poetry, here and there. I am not a poet, but an abuser — that makes all the difference. It is "how you look at it."

But I'm still too ill to write. With best regards to all your family, I am sincerely yours,   AMBROSE BIERCE.

I've been reading your pamphlet on Art Education. You write best when you write most seriously — and your best is very good.

ॐ ॐ ॐ

St. Helena, DEAR BLANCHE,
October 15,
1892.   I send you this picture in exchange for the one that you have — I'm "redeeming" all those with these. But I asked you to return that a long time ago. Please say if you like this; to me it looks like a dude. But I hate the other — the style of it.

It is very good of your father to take so much trouble as to go over and work on that stone. I want the pictures — lithographs — only for economy: so that when persons for whom I do not particularly care want pictures of me I need not bankrupt myself in orders to the photographer. And I do not like photographs anyhow. How long, O Lord, how long am I to wait for that sketch of *you?*

My dear girl, I do not see that folk like your father and me have any just cause of complaint against an unappreciative world; nobody compels us to make things that the world does not want. We merely choose to because the pay, *plus* the satisfaction, exceeds the pay alone that we get from work that the world does want. Then where is our grievance? We get what we prefer when we do good work; for the lesser wage we do easier work. It has never seemed to me that the "unappreciated genius" had a good case to go into court with, and I think he should be promptly non-suited. Inspiration from Heaven is all very fine — the mandate of an attitude or an instinct is good; but when A works for B, yet insists on taking his orders from C, what can he expect? So don't distress your good little heart with compassion — not for me, at least; whenever I tire of pot-boiling, wood-chopping is open to me, and a thousand other honest and profitable employments.

I have noted Gertrude's picture in the Examiner with a peculiar interest. That girl has a bushel of brains, and her father and brother have to look out for her or she will leave them out of sight. I would suggest as a measure of precaution against so monstrous a perversion of natural order that she have her eyes put out. The subjection of women must be maintained.

* * *

Bib and Leigh send love to you. Leigh, I think, is expecting Carlt. I've permitted Leigh to join the band again, and he is very peacocky in his uniform. God bless you.

AMBROSE BIERCE.

MY DEAR BLANCHE,

I am glad you will consent to tolerate the new photograph—all my other friends are desperately delighted with it. I prefer your tolerance.

But I don't like to hear that you have been "ill and blue"; that is a condition which seems more naturally to appertain to me. For, after all, whatever cause you may have for "blueness," you can always recollect that you are *you*, and find a wholesome satisfaction in your identity; whereas I, alas, am *I!*

I'm sure you performed your part of that concert creditably despite the ailing wrist, and wish that I might have added myself to your triumph.

I have been very ill again but hope to get away from here (back to my mountain) before it is time for another attack from my friend the enemy. I shall expect to see you there sometime when my brother and his wife come up. They would hardly dare to come without you.

No, I did not read the criticism you mention — in the *Saturday Review*. Shall send you all the *Saturdays* that I get if you will have them. Anyhow, they will amuse (and sometimes disgust) your father.

I have awful arrears of correspondence, as usual.

The children send love. They had a pleasant visit with Carlt, and we hope he will come again.

May God be very good to you and put it into your heart to write to your uncle often.

Please give my best respects to all Partingtons, jointly and severally.   AMBROSE BIERCE.

DEAR BLANCHE,

Only just a word to say that I have repented of my assent

to your well-meant proposal for your father to write of *me*. If there is anything in my work in letters that engages his interest, or in my *literary* history — that is well enough, and I shall not mind. But "biography" in the other sense is distasteful to me. I never read biographical "stuff" of other writers — of course you know "stuff" is literary slang for "matter" — and think it "beside the question." Moreover, it is distinctly mischievous to letters. It throws no light on one's work, but on the contrary "darkens counsel." The only reason that posterity judges work with some slight approach to accuracy is that posterity knows less, and cares less, about the author's personality. It considers his work as impartially as if it had found it lying on the ground with no footprints about it and no initials on its linen.

My brother is not "fully cognizant" of my history, anyhow — not of the part that is interesting.

So, on the whole, I'll ask that it be not done. It was only my wish to please that made me consent. That wish is no weaker now, but I would rather please otherwise.

I trust that you arrived safe and well, and that your memory of those few stormy days is not altogether disagreeable. Sincerely your friend,   AMBROSE BIERCE.

ॐ ॐ ॐ

MY DEAR BLANCHE,

Returning here from the city this morning, I find your letter. And I had not replied to your last one before that! But *that* was because I hoped to see you at your home. I was unable to do so — I saw no one (but Richard) whom I really wanted to see, and had not an hour unoccupied by work or "business" until this morning. And then — it was Christmas, and my right to act as skeleton at anybody's

Angwin, December 25, 1892.

feast by even so much as a brief call was not clear. I hope my brother will be as forgiving as I know you will be.

When I went down I was just recovering from as severe an attack of illness as I ever had in my life. Please consider unsaid all that I have said in praise of this mountain, its air, water, and everything that is its.

* * *

It was uncommonly nice of Hume to entertain so good an opinion of me; if you had seen him a few days later you would have found a different state of affairs, probably; for I had been exhausting relays of vials of wrath upon him for delinquent diligence in securing copyright for my little story — whereby it is uncopyrighted. I ought to add that he has tried to make reparation, and is apparently contrite to the limit of his penitential capacity.

No, there was no other foundation for the little story than its obvious naturalness and consistency with the sentiments "appropriate to the season." When Christendom is guzzling and gorging and clowning it has not time to cease being cruel; all it can do is to augment its hypocrisy a trifle.

Please don't lash yourself and do various penances any more for your part in the plaguing of poor Russell; he is quite forgotten in the superior affliction sent upon James Whitcomb Riley. *That* seems a matter of genuine public concern, if I may judge by what I heard in town (and I heard little else) and by my letters and "esteemed" (though testy) "contemporaries." Dear, dear, how sensitive people are becoming!

Richard has promised me the Blanchescape that I have so patiently waited for while you were practicing the art of looking pretty in preparation for the sitting, so now I am happy. I shall put you opposite Joaquin Miller, who is now framed and glazed in good shape. I have also your father's sketch of me — that is, I got it and left it in San Francisco to be cleaned if possible; it was in a most unregenerate state of dirt and grease.

Seeing Harry Bigelow's article in the *Wave* on women who write (and it's unpleasantly near to the truth of the matter) I feel almost reconciled to the failure of my gorgeous dream of making a writer of *you*. I wonder if you would have eschewed the harmless, necessary tub and danced upon the broken bones of the innocuous toothbrush. Fancy you with sable nails and a soiled cheek, uttering to the day what God taught in the night! Let us be thankful that the peril is past.

The next time I go to "the Bay" I shall go to 1019 *first*. God bless you for a good girl.   AMBROSE BIERCE.

* * *

[First part of this letter missing.]

* * *

Yes, I know Blackburn Harte has a weakness for the proletariat of letters * * * and doubtless thinks Riley good *because* he is "of the people," peoply. But he will have to endure me as well as he can. You ask my opinion of Burns. He has not, I think, been translated into English, and I do not (that is, I can but *will* not) read that gibberish. I read Burns once — that was once too many times; but happily it was before I knew any better, and so my time, being worthless, was not wasted.

I wish you could be up here this beautiful weather. But I dare say it would rain if you came. In truth, it is "thickening" a trifle just because of my wish. And I wish I *had* given you, for your father, all the facts of my biography from the cradle — downward. When you come again I shall, if you still want them. For I'm worried half to death with requests for them, and when I refuse am no doubt considered surly or worse. And my refusal no longer serves, for the biography men are beginning to write my history from imagination. So the next time I see you I shall give you (orally) that "history of a crime," my life. Then, if your father is still in the notion, he can write it from your notes, and I can answer all future inquiries by enclosing his article.

Do you know? — you will, I think, be glad to know — that I have many more offers for stories at good prices, than I have the health to accept. (For I am less nearly well than I have told you.) Even the *Examiner* has "waked up" (I woke it up) to the situation, and now pays me $20 a thousand words; and my latest offer from New York is $50.

I hardly know why I tell you this unless it is because you tell me of any good fortune that comes to your people, and because you seem to take an interest in my affairs such as nobody else does in just the same unobjectionable and, in fact, agreeable way. I wish you were my "real, sure-enough" niece. But in that case I should expect you to pass all your time at Howell Mountain, with your uncle and cousin. Then I should teach you to write, and you could expound to me the principles underlying the art of being the best girl in the world. Sincerely yours,

AMBROSE BIERCE.

ॐ ॐ ॐ

Angwin,
January 4,
1893.

MY DEAR BLANCHE,

Not hearing from [you] after writing you last week, I fear you are ill—may I not know? I am myself ill, as I feared. On Thursday last I was taken violently ill indeed, and have but just got about. In truth, I'm hardly able to write you, but as I have to go to work on Friday, *sure*, I may as well practice a little on you. And the weather up here is Paradisaical. Leigh and I took a walk this morning in the woods. We scared up a wild deer, but I did not feel able to run it down and present you with its antlers.

I hope you are well, that you are all well. And I hope Heaven will put it into your good brother's heart to send me that picture of the sister who is so much too good for him — or anybody.

In the meantime, and always, God bless you.

AMBROSE BIERCE.

My boy (who has been an angel of goodness to me in my illness) sends his love to you and all your people.

ঌ৹ ঌ৹ ঌ৹

MY DEAR PARTINGTON,

You see the matter is this way. You can't come up here and go back the same day — at least that would give you but about an hour here. You must remain over night. Now I put it to you — how do you think I'd feel if you came and remained over night and I, having work to do, should have to leave you to your own devices, mooning about a place that has nobody to talk to? When a fellow comes a long way to see me I want to see a good deal of him, however *he* may feel about it. It is not the same as if he lived in the same bailiwick and "dropped in." That is why, in the present state of my health and work, I ask all my friends to give me as long notice of their comingas possible. I'm sure you'll say I am right, inasmuch as certain work if undertaken must be done by the time agreed upon.

Angwin, Cal., January 14, 1893.

My relations with Danziger are peculiar — as any one's relations with him must be. In the matter of which you wished to speak I could say nothing. For this I must ask you to believe there are reasons. It would not have been fair not to let you know, before coming, that I would not talk of him.

I thought, though, that you would probably come up to-day if I wrote you. Well, I should like you to come and pass a week with me. But if you come for a day I naturally want it to be an "off" day with me. Sincerely yours,

AMBROSE BIERCE.

ᲐᎦᎨ ᲐᎦᎨ ᲐᎦᎨ

Angwin,
January 23,
1893. MY DEAR BLANCHE,

I should have written you sooner; it has been ten whole days since the date of your last letter. But I have not been in the mood of letter writing, and am prepared for mal-edictions from all my neglected friends but you. My health is better. Yesterday I returned from Napa, where I passed twenty-six hours, buried, most of the time, in fog; but apparently it has not harmed me. The weather here remains heavenly. * * *

If I grow better in health I shall in time feel able to ex-tend my next foray into the Lowlands as far as Oakland and Berkeley.

Here are some fronds of maiden-hair fern that I have just brought in. The first wild flowers of the season are begin-ning to venture out and the manzanitas are a sight to see.

With warmest regards to all your people, I am, as ever, your most unworthy uncle,   AMBROSE BIERCE.

ᲐᎦᎨ ᲐᎦᎨ ᲐᎦᎨ

Angwin,
February 5,
1893. MY DEAR BLANCHE,

What an admirable reporter you would be! Your account of the meeting with Miller in the restaurant and of the "entertainment" are amusing no end. * * * By the way,

I observe a trooly offle "attack" on me in the Oakland *Times* of the 3rd (I think) * * * (I know of course it means me — I always know that when they pull out of their glowing minds that old roasted chestnut about "tearing down" but not "building up" — that is to say, effacing one imposture without giving them another in place of it.) The amusing part of the business is that he points a contrast between me and Realf (God knows there's unlikeness enough) quite unconscious of the fact that it is I and no other who have "built up" Realf's reputation as a poet — published his work, and paid him for it, when nobody else would have it; repeatedly pointed out its greatness, and when he left that magnificent crown of sonnets behind him protested that posterity would know California better by the incident of his death than otherwise — not a soul, until now, concurring in my view of the verses. Believe me, my trade is not without its humorous side.

Leigh and I went down to the waterfall yesterday. It was almost grand — greater than I had ever seen it — and I took the liberty to wish that you might see it in that state. My wish must have communicated itself, somehow, though imperfectly, to Leigh, for as I was indulging it he expressed the same wish with regard to Richard.

I wish too that you might be here to-day to see the swirls of snow. It is falling rapidly, and I'm thinking that this letter will make its way down the mountain to-morrow morning through a foot or two of it. Unluckily, it has a nasty way of turning to rain.

My health is very good now, and Leigh and I take long walks. And after the rains we look for Indian arrow-heads in the plowed fields and on the gravel bars of the creek. My collection is now great; but I fear I shall tire of the fad before completing it. One in the country must have a fad or die of dejection and oxidation of the faculties. How happy is he who can make a fad of his work!

By the way, my New York publishers (The United States Book Company) have failed, owing me a pot of money, of which I shall probably get nothing. I'm beginning to cherish an impertinent curiosity to know what Heaven means to do to me next. If your function as one of the angels gives you a knowledge of such matters please betray your trust and tell me where I'm to be hit, and how hard.

But this is an intolerable deal of letter.

With best regards to all good Partingtons — and I think there are no others — I remain your affectionate uncle by adoption,   AMBROSE BIERCE.

Leigh has brought in some manzanita blooms which I shall try to enclose. But they'll be badly smashed.

✺ ✺ ✺

My DEAR BLANCHE,

Angwin,
February 14,
1893.

I thank you many times for the picture, which is a monstrous good picture, whatever its shortcomings as a portrait may be. On the authority of the great art critic, Leigh Bierce, I am emboldened to pronounce some of the work in it equal to Gribayedoff at his best; and that, according to the g. a. c. aforesaid, is to exhaust eulogium. But — it isn't altogether the Blanche that I know, as I know her. Maybe it is the hat — I should prefer you hatless, and so less at the mercy of capricious fortune. Suppose hats were to "go out" — I tremble to think of what would happen to that gorgeous superstructure which now looks so beautiful. O, well, when I come down I shall drag you to the hateful photographer and get something that looks quite like you — and has no other value.

And I mean to "see Oakland and die" pretty soon. I have not dared go when the weather was bad. It promises well now, but I am to have visitors next Sunday, so must stay at home. God and the weather bureau willing, you may be bothered with me the Saturday or Sunday after. We shall see.

I hope your father concurs in my remarks on picture "borders" — I did not think of him until the remarks had been written, or I should have assured myself of his practice before venturing to utter my mind o' the matter. If it were not for him and Gertrude and the *Wave* I should snarl again, anent "half-tones," which I abhor. Hume tried to get me to admire his illustrations, but I would not, so far as the process is concerned, and bluntly told him he would not get your father's best work that way.

If you were to visit the Mountain now I should be able to show you a redwood forest (newly discovered) and a picturesque gulch to match.

The wild flowers are beginning to put up their heads to look for you, and my collection of Indian antiquities is yearning to have you see it.

Please convey my thanks to Richard for the picture — the girlscape — and my best regards to your father and all the others.   Sincerely your friend,

AMBROSE BIERCE.

My dear Blanche,

I'm very sorry indeed that I cannot be in Oakland Thursday evening to see you "in your glory," arrayed, doubtless, like a lily of the field. However glorious you may be in public, though, I fancy I should like you better as you used to be out at camp. Angwin, February 21, 1893.

Well, I mean to see you on Saturday afternoon if you are

at home, and think I shall ask you to be my guide to Grizzlyville; for surely I shall never be able to find the wonderful new house alone. So if your mamma will let you go out there with me I promise to return you to her in-ɔtead of running away with you. And, possibly, weather permitting, we can arrange for a Sunday in the redwoods or on the hills. Or don't your folks go out any more o' Sundays?

Please give my thanks to your mother for the kind invitation to put up at your house; but I fear that would be impossible. I shall have to be where people can call on me — and such a disreputable crowd as my friends are would ruin the Partingtonian reputation for respectability. In your new neighborhood you will all be very proper — which you could hardly be with a procession of pirates and vagrants pulling at your door-bell.

So — if God is good — I shall call on you Saturday afternoon. In the meantime and always be thou happy — thou and thine. Your unworthy uncle,　　AMBROSE BIERCE.

ɔ⊕ ɔ⊕ ɔ⊕

Angwin,
March 18,
1893.

MY DEAR BLANCHE,

It is good to have your letters again. If you will not let me teach you my trade of writing stories it is right that you practice your own of writing letters. You are mistress of that. Byron's letters to Moore are dull in comparison with yours to me. Some allowance, doubtless, must be made for my greater need of your letters than of Byron's. For, truth to tell, I've been a trifle dispirited and noncontent. In that mood I peremptorily resigned from the *Examiner,* for one thing — and permitted myself to be coaxed back by Hearst, for another. My other follies I shall not tell you. * * *

We had six inches of snow up here and it has rained

steadily ever since — more than a week. And the fog is of superior opacity — quite peerless that way. It is still raining and fogging. Do you wonder that your unworthy uncle has come perilously and alarmingly near to loneliness? Yet I have the companionship, at meals, of one of your excellent sex, from San Francisco. * * *

Truly, I should like to attend one of your at-homes, but I fear it must be a long time before I venture down there again. But when this brumous visitation is past I can *look* down, and that assists the imagination to picture you all in your happy (I hope) home. But if that woolly wolf, Joaquin Miller, doesn't keep outside the fold I *shall* come down and club him soundly. I quite agree with your mother that his flattery will spoil you. You said I would spoil Phyllis, and now, you bad girl, you wish to be spoiled yourself. Well, you can't eat four Millerine oranges.—My love to all your family.

AMBROSE BIERCE.

&ð &ð &ð

MY DEAR PARTINGTON,

I am very glad indeed to get the good account of Leigh that you give me. I've feared that he might be rather a bore to you, but you make me easy on that score. Also I am pleased that you think he has a sufficient "gift" to do something in the only direction in which he seems to care to go.

He is anxious to take the place at the *Examiner*, and his uncle thinks that would be best — if they will give it him. I'm a little reluctant for many reasons, but there are considerations — some of them going to the matter of character and disposition — which point to that as the best arrangement. The boy needs discipline, control, and work. He needs to learn by experience that life is not all beer and

Angwin,
March 26,
1893.

skittles. Of course you can't quite know him as I do. As to his earning anything on the *Examiner* or elsewhere, that cuts no figure — he'll spend everything he can get his fingers on anyhow; but I feel that he ought to have the advantage of a struggle for existence where the grass is short and the soil stony.

Well, I shall let him live down there somehow, and see what can be done with him. There's a lot of good in him, and a lot of the other thing, naturally.

I hope Hume has, or will, put you in authority in the *Post* and give you a decent salary. He seems quite enthusiastic about the *Post* and — about you.

With sincere regards to Mrs. Partington and all the Partingtonettes, I am very truly yours,   AMBROSE BIERCE.

Angwin, April 10, 1893.

MY DEAR PARTINGTON,

If you are undertaking to teach my kid (which, unless it is entirely agreeable to you, you must not do) I hope you will regard him as a pupil whose tuition is to be paid for like any other pupil. And you should, I think, name the price. Will you kindly do so?

Another thing. Leigh tells me you paid him for something he did for the *Wave*. That is not right. While you let him work with you, and under you, his work belongs to you — is a part of yours. I mean the work that he does in your shop for the *Wave*.

I don't wish to feel that you are bothering with him for nothing—will you not tell me your notion of what I should pay you?

I fancy you'll be on the *Examiner* pretty soon—if you wish.

With best regards to your family I am sincerely yours,

AMBROSE BIERCE.

My dear Blanche,

As I was writing to your father I was, of course, strongly impressed with a sense of *you;* for you are an intrusive kind of creature, coming into one's consciousness in the most lawless way — Phyllis-like. (Phyllis is my "type and example" of lawlessness, albeit I'm devoted to her — a Phyllistine, as it were.) Angwin, April 10, 1893.

Leigh sends me a notice (before the event) of your concert. I hope it was successful. Was it?

It rains or snows here all the time, and the mountain struggles in vain to put on its bravery of leaf and flower. When this kind of thing stops I'm going to put in an application for you to come up and get your bad impressions of the place effaced. It is insupportable that my earthly paradise exist in your memory as a "bad eminence," like Satan's primacy.

I'm sending you the *New England Magazine* — perhaps I have sent it already — and a *Harper's Weekly* with a story by Mrs. * * * , who is a sort of pupil of mine. She used to do bad work — does now sometimes; but she will do great work by-and-by.

I wish you had not got that notion that you cannot learn to write. You see I'd like you to do *some* art work that I can understand and enjoy. I wonder why it is that no note or combination of notes can be struck out of a piano that will touch me — give me an emotion of any kind. It is not wholly due to my ignorance and bad ear, for other instruments — the violin, organ, zither, guitar, etc., sometimes affect me profoundly. Come, read me the riddle if you know. What have I done that I should be inaccessible to your music? I know it is good; I can hear that it is, but not feel that it is. Therefore to me it is not.

Now that, you will confess, is a woeful state — "most tolerable and not to be endured." Will you not cultivate some art within the scope of my capacity? Do you think you could learn to walk on a wire (if it lay on the ground)? Can you not ride three horses at once if they are suitably dead? Or swallow swords? Really, you should have some way to entertain your uncle.

True, you can talk, but you never get the chance; I always "have the floor." Clearly you must learn to write, and I mean to get Miller to teach you how to be a poet.

I hope you will write occasionally to me, — letter-writing is an art that you do excel in — as I in "appreciation" of your excellence in it.

Do you see my boy? I hope he is good, and diligent in his work.   * * *

You must write to me or I shall withdraw my avuncular relation to you.

With good will to all your people — particularly Phyllis — I am sincerely your friend,   AMBROSE BIERCE.

ᔆᓛ ᔆᓛ ᔆᓛ

Angwin, Calif., MY DEAR PARTINGTON,
April 16,
1893.   I think you wrong. On your own principle, laid down in your letter, that "every man has a right to the full value of his labor" — pardon me, good Englishman, I meant "laboUr" — you have a right to your wage for the laboᵘr of teaching Leigh. And what work would *he* get to do but for you?

I can't hold you and inject shekels into your pocket, but if the voice of remonstrance has authority to enter at your ear without a ticket I pray you to show it hospitality.

Leigh doubtless likes to see his work in print, but I hope you will not let him put anything out until it is as good as he can make it — nor then if it is not good *enough*. And that whether he signs it or not. I have talked to him about the relation of conscience to lab — work, but I don't know if my talk all came out at the other ear.

O — that bad joke o' mine. Where do you and Richard expect to go when death do you part? You were neither of you present that night on the dam, nor did I know either of you. Blanche, thank God, retains the old-time reverence for truth: it was to her that I said it. Richard evidently dreamed it, and you — you've been believing that confounded *Wave!* Sincerely yours,   AMBROSE BIERCE.

〜 〜 〜

MY DEAR BLANCHE,

I take a few moments from work to write you in order (mainly) to say that your letter of March 31st did not go astray, as you seem to fear — though why *you* should care if it did I can't conjecture. The loss to me — that is probably what would touch your compassionate heart.

Angwin, April 18, 1893.

So you *will* try to write. That is a good girl. I'm almost sure you can — not, of course, all at once, but by-and-by. And if not, what matter? You are not of the sort, I am sure, who would go on despite everything, determined to succeed by dint of determining to succeed.

* * *

We are blessed with the most amiable of all conceivable weathers up here, and the wild flowers are putting up their heads everywhere to look for you. Lying in their graves last autumn, they overheard (*under*heard) your promise to come in the spring, and it has stimulated and cheered them to a vigorous growth.

I'm sending you some more papers. Don't think yourself obliged to read all the stuff I send you — *I* don't read it.

Condole with me — I have just lost another publisher — by failure. Schulte, of Chicago, publisher of "The Monk" etc., has "gone under," I hear. Danziger and I have not had a cent from him. I put out three books in a year, and lo! each one brings down a publisher's gray hair in sorrow to the grave! for Langton, of "Black Beetles," came to grief — that is how Danziger got involved. "O that mine enemy would *publish* one of my books!"

I am glad to hear of your success at your concert. If I could have reached you you should have had the biggest basket of pretty vegetables that was ever handed over the footlights. I'm sure you merited it all — what do you *not* merit?

Your father gives me good accounts of my boy. He *must* be doing well, I think, by the way he neglects all my commissions.

Enclosed you will find my contribution to the Partington art gallery, with an autograph letter from the artist. You can hang them in any light you please and show them to Richard. He will doubtless be pleased to note how the latent genius of his boss has burst into bloom.

I have been wading in the creek this afternoon for pure love of it; the gravel looked so clean under the water. I was for the moment at least ten years younger than your father. To whom, and to all the rest of your people, my sincere regards, Your uncle,　　AMBROSE BIERCE.

✿ ✿ ✿

Angwin, Cala.,　MY DEAR BLANCHE,
April 26,
1893.　　　　　　　* * *

I accept your sympathy for my misfortunes in publishing. It serves me right (I don't mean the sympathy does) for publishing. I should have known that if a publisher cannot beat an author otherwise, or is too honest to do so, he will do it by failing. Once in London a publisher gave me a check dated two days ahead, and then (the only thing he could do to make the check worthless —ate a pork pie and died. That was the late John Camden Hotten, to whose business and virtues my present London publishers, Chatto and Windus, have succeeded. They have not failed, and they refuse pork pie, but they deliberately altered the title of my book.

All this for your encouragement in "learning to write." Writing books is a noble profession; it has not a shade of selfishness in it — nothing worse than conceit.

O yes, you shall have your big basket of flowers if ever I catch you playing in public. I wish I could give you the carnations, lilies-of-the-valley, violets, and first-of-the-season sweet peas now on my table. They came from down near you — which fact they are trying triumphantly and as hard as they can to relate in fragrance.

I trust your mother is well of her cold — that you are all well and happy, and that Phyllis will not forget me. And may the good Lord bless you regularly every hour of every day for your merit, and every minute of every hour as a special and particular favor to   Your uncle,

AMBROSE BIERCE.

⁂

MY DEAR BLANCHE,

I accept with pleasure your evidence that the Piano is not Berkeley, as black as I have painted, albeit the logical inference is October 2, that I'm pretty black myself. Indubitably I'm "in outer 1893. darkness," and can only say to you: "Lead, kindly light."

Thank you for the funny article on the luxury question — from the funny source. But you really must not expect me to answer it, nor show you wherein it is "wrong." I cannot discern the expediency of you having any "views" at all in those matters — even correct ones. If I could have my way you should think of more profitable things than the (conceded) "wrongness" of a world which is the habitat of a wrongheaded and wronghearted race of irreclaimable savages. * * * When woman "broadens her sympathies" they become annular. Don't.

Cosgrave came over yesterday for a "stroll," but as he had a dinner engagement to keep before going home, he was in gorgeous gear. So I kindly hoisted him atop of Grizzly Peak and sent him back across the Bay in a condition impossible to describe, save by the aid of a wet dishclout for illustration.

Please ask your father when and where he wants me to sit for the portrait. If that picture is not sold, and ever comes into my possession, I shall propose to swap it for yours. I have always wanted to lay thievish hands on that, and would even like to come by it honestly. But what under the sun would I do with either that or mine? Fancy me packing large paintings about to country hotels and places of last resort!

Leigh is living with me now. Poor chap, the death of his aunt has made him an orphan. I feel a profound compassion for any one whom an untoward fate compels to live with *me*. However, such a one is sure to be a good deal alone, which is a mitigation.

With good wishes for all your people, I am sincerely yours,

AMBROSE BIERCE.

❧ ❧ ❧

Berkeley,
December 27,
1893.

MY DEAR BLANCHE,

I'm sending you (by way of pretext for writing you) a

magazine that I asked Richard to take to you last evening, but which he forgot. There's an illustrated article on gargoyles and the like, which will interest you. Some of the creatures are delicious — more so than I had the sense to perceive when I saw them alive on Notre Dame.

I want to thank you too for the beautiful muffler before I take to my willow chair, happy in the prospect of death. For at this hour, 10:35 p. m., I "have on" a very promising case of asthma. If I come out of it decently alive in a week or so I shall go over to your house and see the finished portrait if it is "still there," like the flag in our national anthem. Sincerely yours,

AMBROSE BIERCE.

❧ ❧ ❧

MY DEAR BLANCHE,

If you are not utterly devoured by mosquitoes perhaps you'll go to the postoffice and get this. In that hope I write, not without a strong sense of the existence of the clerks in the Dead Letter Office at Washington. Oakland, July 31, 1894.

I hope you are (despite the mosquitoes) having "heaps" of rest and happiness. As to me, I have only just recovered sufficiently to be out, and "improved the occasion" by going to San Francisco yesterday and returning on the 11:15 boat. I saw Richard, and he seemed quite solemn at the thought of the dispersal of his family to the four winds.

I have a joyous letter from Leigh dated "on the road," nearing Yosemite. He has been passing through the storied land of Bret Harte, and is permeated with a sense of its beauty and romance. When shall you return? May I hope, then, to see you? Sincerely yours,

AMBROSE BIERCE.

P. S. Here are things that I cut out for memoranda. On

second thought *I* know all that; so send them to you for the betterment of your mind and heart.   B.

მ⟩ მ⟩ მ⟩

San Jose,
October 17,
1894.
My dear Blanche,

Your kindly note was among a number which I put into my pocket at the postoffice and forgot until last evening when I returned from Oakland. (I dared remain up there only a few hours, and the visit did me no good.)

Of course I should have known that your good heart would prompt the wish to hear from your patient, but I fear I was a trifle misanthropic all last week, and indisposed to communicate with my species.

I came here on Monday of last week, and the change has done me good. I have no asthma and am slowly getting back my strength.

Leigh and Ina Peterson passed Sunday with me, and Leigh recounted his adventures in the mountains. I had been greatly worried about him; it seems there was abundant reason. The next time he comes I wish he would bring you. It is lovely down here. Perhaps you and Katie can come some time, and I'll drive you all over the valley — if you care to drive.

If I continue well I shall remain here or hereabout; if not I don't know where I shall go. Probably into the Santa Cruz mountains or to Gilroy. If I could have my way I'd live at Piedmont.

Do you know I lost Pin the Reptile? I brought him along in my bicycle bag (I came the latter half of the way bikeback) and the ungrateful scoundrel wormed himself out and took to the weeds just before we got to San Jose. So I've nothing to lavish my second-childhoodish affection upon — nothing but just myself.

My permanent address is Oakland, as usual, but *you* may address me here at San Jose if you will be so good as to address me anywhere. Please do, and tell me of your triumphs and trials at the Conservatory of Music. I do fervently hope it may prove a means of prosperity to you, for, behold, you are The Only Girl in the World Who Merits Prosperity!

Please give my friendly regards to your people; and so — Heaven be good to you.   AMBROSE BIERCE.

O, BEST OF POETS,

How have you the heart to point out what you deem an imperfection in those lines. Upon my soul, I swear they are faultless, and "moonlight" is henceforth and forever a rhyme to "delight." Also, likewise, moreover and furthermore, a ——— is henceforth ———; and ——— are forever ———; and to ——— shall be ———; and so forth. You have established new canons of literary criticism—more liberal ones—and death to the wretch who does not accept them! Ah, I always knew you were a revolutionist.

San Jose, October 28, 1894.

Yes, I am in better health, worse luck! For I miss the beef-teaing expeditions more than you can by trying.

By the way, if you again encounter your fellow practitioner, Mrs. Hirshberg, please tell her what has become of her patient, and that I remember her gratefully.

It is not uninteresting to me to hear of your progress in your art, albeit I am debarred from entrance into the temple where it is worshiped. After all, art finds its best usefulness in its reaction upon the character; and in that work I can trace your proficiency in the art that you love. As you become a better artist you grow a nicer girl, and if your music does not cause my tympana to move themselves aright, yet the niceness is not without its effect upon the soul o' me. So I'm not so *very* inert a clod, after all.

No, Leigh has not infected me with the exploring fad. I exhausted my capacity in that way years before I had the advantage of his acquaintance and the contagion of his example. But I don't like to think of that miserable mountain sitting there and grinning in the consciousness of having beaten the Bierce family.

So—apropos of my brother—*I* am "odd" after a certain fashion! My child, that is blasphemy. You grow hardier every day of your life, and you'll end as a full colonel yet, and challenge Man to mortal combat in true Stetsonian style. Know thy place, thou atom!

Speaking of colonels reminds me that one of the most eminent of the group had the assurance to write me, asking for an "audience" to consult about a benefit that she — *she*! — is getting up for my friend Miss * * *, a glorious writer and eccentric old maid whom you do not know. * * * evidently wants more notoriety and proposes to shine by Miss * * * light. I was compelled to lower the temperature of the situation with a letter curtly courteous. Not even to assist Miss * * * shall my name be mixed up with those of that gang. But of course all that does not amuse you.

I wish I could have a chat with you. I speak to nobody but my chambermaid and the waiter at my restaurant. By the time I see you I shall have lost the art of speech altogether and shall communicate with you by the sign language.

God be good to you and move you to write to me sometimes.   Sincerely your friend,

AMBROSE BIERCE.

[First part of this letter missing.]

* * *

You may, I think, expect my assistance in choosing between (or among) your suitors next month, early. I propose to try living in Oakland again for a short time beginning about then. But I shall have much to do the first few days — possibly in settling my earthly affairs for it is my determination to be hanged for killing all those suitors. That seems to me the simplest way of disembarrassing you. As to me — it is the "line of least resistance" — unless they fight.

* * *

So you have been ill. You must not be ill, my child — it disturbs my Marcus Aurelian tranquillity, and is most selfishly inconsiderate of you.

Mourn with me: the golden leaves of my poplars are now underwheel. I sigh for the perennial eucalyptus leaf of Piedmont.

I hope you are all well. Sincerely your friend,

AMBROSE BIERCE.

Since writing you yesterday, dear Blanche, I have observed that the benefit to * * * is not abandoned — it is to occur in the evening of the 26th, at Golden Gate Hall, San Francisco. I recall your kind offer to act for me in any way that I might wish to assist Miss * * *. Now, I will not have my name connected with anything that the * * * woman and her sister-in-evidence may do for their own glorification, but I enclose a Wells, Fargo & Co. money order for all the money I can presently afford — wherewith you may do as you will; buy tickets, or hand it to the treasurer in your own name. I know Miss * * * must be awfully needy to

San Jose, November 20, 1894.

accept a benefit — you have no idea how sensitive and suspicious and difficult she is. She is almost impossible. But there are countless exactions on my lean purse, and I must do the rest with my pen. So — I thank you.

Sincerely your friend,
AMBROSE BIERCE.

❧ ❧ ❧

18 Iowa Circle,
Washington, D. C.,
January 1,
1901.

DEAR STERLING,

This is just a hasty note to acknowledge receipt of your letter and the poems. I hope to reach those pretty soon and give them the attention which I am sure they will prove to merit — which I cannot do now. By the way, I wonder why most of you youngsters so persistently tackle the sonnet. For the same reason, I suppose, that a fellow always wants to make his first appearance on the stage in the rôle of "Hamlet." It is just the holy cheek of you.

Yes, Leigh prospers fairly well, and I — well, I don't know if it is prosperity; it is a pretty good time.

I suppose I shall have to write to that old scoundrel Grizzly,* to give him my new address, though I supposed he had it; and the old one would do, anyhow. Now that his cub has returned he probably doesn't care for the other plantigrades of his kind.

Thank you for telling me so much about some of our companions and companionesses of the long ago. I fear that not all my heart was in my baggage when I came over here. There's a bit of it, for example, out there by that little lake in the hills.

So I may have a photograph of one of your pretty sisters. Why, of course I want it — I want the entire five of them; their pictures, I mean. If you had been a nice fellow you

*Albert Bierce.

would have let me know them long ago. And how about that other pretty girl, your infinitely better half? You might sneak into the envelope a little portrait of *her*, lest I forget, lest I forget. But I've not yet forgotten.

The new century's best blessings to the both o' you.

AMBROSE BIERCE.

P. S. — In your studies of poetry have you dipped into Stedman's new "American Anthology"? It is the most notable collection of American verse that has been made — on the whole, a book worth having. In saying so I rather pride myself on my magnanimity; for of course I don't think he has done as well by me as he might have done. That, I suppose, is what every one thinks who happens to be alive to think it. So I try to be in the fashion.   A. B.

～ ～ ～

MY DEAR STERLING,

I've been a long while getting to your verses, but there were many reasons — including a broken rib. They are pretty good verses, with here and there *very* good lines. I'd a strong temptation to steal one or two for my "Passing Show," but I knew what an avalanche of verses it would bring down upon me from other poets — as every mention of a new book loads my mail with new books for a month.

18 Iowa Circle,
Washington, D. C.,
January 19,
1901.

If I ventured to advise you I should recommend to you the simple, ordinary meters and forms native to our language.

I await the photograph of the pretty sister — don't fancy I've forgotten.

It is 1 a. m. and I'm about to drink your health in a glass of Riesling and eat it in a pâte.

My love to Grizzly if you ever see him. Yours ever,

A. B.

Washington, D. C.,
January 23,
1901. MY DEAR DOYLE,

Your letter of the 16th has just come and as I am waiting at my office (where I seldom go) I shall amuse myself by replying "to onct." See here, I don't purpose that your attack on poor Morrow's book shall become a "continuous performance," nor even an "annual ceremony." It is not "rot." It is not "filthy." It does not "suggest bed-pans,"— at least it did not to me, and I'll wager something that Morrow never thought of them. Observe and consider: If his hero and heroine had been man and wife, the bed-pan would have been there, just the same; yet you would not have thought of it. Every reader would have been touched by the husband's devotion. A physician has to do with many unpleasant things; whom do his ministrations disgust? A trained nurse lives in an atmosphere of bed-pans — to whom is her presence or work suggestive of them? I'm thinking of the heroic Father Damien and his lepers; do you dwell upon the rotting limbs and foul distortions of his unhappy charges? Is not his voluntary martyrdom one of the sanest, cleanest, most elevating memories in all history? Then it is *not* the bed-pan necessity that disgusts you; it is something else. It is the fact that the hero of the story, being neither physician, articled nurse, nor certificated husband, nevertheless performed *their* work. He ministered to the helpless in a natural way without authority from church or college, quite irregular and improper and all that. My noble critic, there speaks in your blood the Untamed Philistine. You were not caught young enough. You came into letters and art with all your beastly conventionalities in full mastery of you. Take a purge. Forget that there are Philistines. Forget that they have put their abominable pantalettes upon the legs of Nature. Forget that their code of morality and manners (it stinks worse than a bed-pan) does *not* exist in the serene altitude of great art, toward which you have set your toes and into which I want you to climb. I know about this thing. I, too, tried to rise with all that dead weight dragging at my feet. Well, I could not — now I could if I cared to. In my mind I do. It is not freedom of act — not freedom of living, for which I contend, but freedom of thought, of mind, of spirit; the freedom to see in the horrible laws, prejudices, custom, conventionalities of the multitude, something good for them, but of no value to you *in your art*. In your life and conduct defer to as much of it as you will (you'll find it convenient to defer to a whole lot), but in your mind and art let not the Philistine enter, nor even speak a word through the keyhole. My own chief objection to Morrow's story is (as I apprised him) its unnaturalness. He did not dare to follow the logical course of his narrative. He was too cowardly (or had too keen an eye upon his market of prudes) to make hero and heroine join in the holy bonds of *bed*lock, as they naturally, inevitably and rightly would have done long before she was able to be about. I daresay that, too, would have seemed to you "filthy," without the parson and his fee. When you analyze your objection to the story (as I have tried to do for you) you will find that it all crystallizes into that — the absence of the parson. I don't envy you your view of the matter, and I really don't think you greatly enjoy it yourself. I forgot to say: Suppose they had been two men, two partners in hunting, mining, or exploring, as frequently occurs. Would the bed-pan suggestion have come to you? Did it come to you when you read of the slow, but not uniform, starvation of Greeley's party in the arctic? Of course not. Then it is a matter, not of bed-pans, but of sex-exposure (unauthorized by the church), of prudery — of that artificial thing, the "sense of shame," of which the great Greeks knew nothing; of which the great Japanese know nothing; of which Art knows nothing. Dear Doctor, do you really put trousers on your piano-legs? Does your indecent intimacy with your mirror make you blush?

There, there's the person whom I've been waiting for (I'm to take her to dinner, and I'm not married to even so much of her as her little toe) has come; and until you offend again, you are immune from the switch. May all your brother Philistines have to "Kiss the place to make it well."

Pan is dead! Long live Bed-Pan!

Yours ever,

AMBROSE BIERCE.

๑๑ ๑๑ ๑๑

Washington,
February 17,
1901.

MY DEAR STERLING,

I send back the poems, with a few suggestions. You grow great so rapidly that I shall not much longer dare to touch your work. I mean that.

Your criticisms of Stedman's Anthology are just. But equally just ones can be made of any anthology. None of them can suit any one. I fancy Stedman did not try to "live up" to his standard, but to make *representative*, though not always the *best*, selections. It would hardly do to leave out Whitman, for example. *We* may not like him; thank God, we don't; but many others — the big fellows too — do; and in England he is thought great. And then Stedman has the bad luck to know a lot of poets personally — many bad poets. Put yourself in his place. Would you leave out me if you honestly thought my work bad?

In any compilation we will all miss some of our favor-ites — and find some of the public's favorites. You miss from Whittier "Joseph Sturge" — I the sonnet "Forgive-ness," and so forth. Alas, there is no universal standard!

Thank you for the photographs. Miss * * * is a pretty girl, truly, and has the posing instinct as well. She has the place of honor on my mantel. * * * But what scurvy knave has put the stage-crime into her mind? If you know that life as I do you will prefer that she die, poor girl.

It is no trouble, but a pleasure, to go over your verses — I am as proud of your talent as if I'd made it.

Sincerely yours,

[over]   AMBROSE BIERCE.

About the rhymes in a sonnet:

"Regular," or Italian form (Petrarch):	"English" form (Shakspear's):	Modern English
1	1	1
2	2	2
2	1	2
1	2	1
1	3	1
2	4	2
2	3	2
1	4	1
3	5	Two or three rhymes; any arrangement
4	6	
5	5	
3	6	
4	7	
5	7	

There are good reasons for preferring the regular Italian form created by Petrarch — who knew a thing or two; and sometimes good reasons for another arrangement — of the sestet rhymes. If one should sacrifice a great thought to be like Petrarch one would not resemble him.   A. B.

Washington, D. C.,
May 2,
1901.
My dear Sterling,

I am sending to the "Journal" your splendid poem on Memorial Day. Of course I can't say what will be its fate. I am not even personally acquainted with the editor of the department to which it goes. But if he has not the brains to like it he is to send it back and I'll try to place it elsewhere. It is great — great! — the loftiest note that you have struck and *held*.

Maybe I owe you a lot of letters. I don't know—my correspondence all in arrears and I've not the heart to take it up.

Thank you for your kind words of sympathy.* I'm hit harder than any one can guess from the known facts — am a bit broken and gone gray of it all.

But I remember you asked the title of a book of synonyms. It is "Roget's Thesaurus," a good and useful book.

The other poems I will look up soon and consider. I've made no alterations in the "Memorial Day" except to insert the omitted stanza. Sincerely yours,

AMBROSE BIERCE.

Washington,
May 9,
1901.
My dear Sterling,

I send the poems with suggestions. There's naught to say about 'em that I've not said of your other work. Your "growth in grace" (and other poetic qualities) is something wonderful. You are leaving my other "pupils" so far behind that they are no longer "in it." Seriously, you "promise" better than any of the new men in our literature — and perform better than all but Markham in his lucid intervals, alas, too rare.

Sincerely yours,

AMBROSE BIERCE.

*Concerning the death of his son Leigh.

My dear Sterling,

I enclose a proof of the poem* — all marked up. The poem was offered to the Journal, but to the wrong editor. I would not offer it to him in whose department it could be used, for he once turned down some admirable verses of my friend Scheffauer which I sent him. I'm glad the Journal is *not* to have it, for it now goes into the Washington Post — and the Post into the best houses here and elsewhere — a good, clean, unyellow paper. I'll send you some copies with the poem.

Washington, May 22, 1901.

I think my marks are intelligible — I mean my *re*marks. Perhaps you'll not approve all, or anything, that I did to the poem; I'll only ask you to endure. When you publish in covers you can restore to the original draft if you like. I had not time (after my return from New York) to get your approval and did the best and the least I could.

* * *

My love to your pretty wife and sister. Let me know how hard you hate me for monkeying with your sacred lines.

Sincerely yours,

Ambrose Bierce.

Yes, your poem recalled my "Invocation" as I read it; but it is better, and not too much like — hardly like at all except in the "political" part. Both, in that, are characterized, I think, by decent restraint. How * * * would, at those places, have ranted and chewed soap! — a superior quality of soap, I confess. A. B.

My dear Sterling,

I am glad my few words of commendation were not unpleasing to you. I meant them all and more. You ought to

1825 Nineteenth St., N. W., Washington, D. C., June 30, 1901.

*"Memorial Day."

have praise, seeing that it is all you got. The "Post," like most other newspapers, "don't pay for poetry." What a damning confession! It means that the public is as insensible to poetry as a pig to — well, to poetry. To any sane mind such a poem as yours is worth more than all the other contents of a newspaper for a year.

I've not found time to consider your "bit of blank" yet — at least not as carefully as it probably merits.

My relations with the present editor of the Examiner are not unfriendly, I hope, but they are too slight to justify me in suggesting anything to him, or even drawing his attention to anything. I hoped you would be sufficiently "enterprising" to get your poem into the paper if you cared to have it there. I wrote Dr. Doyle about you. He is a dear fellow and you should know each other. As to Scheffauer, he is another. If you want him to see your poem why not send it to him? But the last I heard he was very ill. I'm rather anxious to hear more about him.

It was natural to enclose the stamps, but I won't have it so — so there! as the women say.

Sincerely yours,

AMBROSE BIERCE.

૭◑ ૭◑ ૭◑

1825 Nineteenth St., N. W., Washington, D. C., July 15, 1901.

MY DEAR STERLING,

Here is the bit of blank. When are we to see the book? Needless question — when you can spare the money to pay for publication, I suppose, if by that time you are ambitious to achieve public inattention. That's my notion of encouragement — I like to cheer up the young author as he sets his face toward "the peaks of song."

Say, that photograph of the pretty sister — the one with a downward slope of the eyes — is all faded out. That is a real misfortune: it reduces the sum of human happiness hereabout. Can't you have one done in fast colors and let me have it? The other is all right, but that is not the one that I like the better for my wall. Sincerely yours,

AMBROSE BIERCE.

ᴓ᷐ ᴓ᷐ ᴓ᷐

MY DEAR STERLING,

I enclose the poems with a few suggestions. They require little criticism of the sort that would be "helpful." As to their merit I think them good, but not great. I suppose you do not expect to write great things every time. Yet in the body of your letter (of Oct. 22) you do write greatly — and say that the work is "egoistic" and "unprintable." If it* were addressed to another person than myself I should say that it is "printable" exceedingly. Call it what you will, but let me tell you it will probably be long before you write anything better than some — many — of these stanzas.

The Olympia, Washington, D. C., December 16, 1901.

You ask if you have correctly answered your own questions. Yes; in four lines of your running comment:

"I suppose that I'd do the greater good in the long run by making my work as good poetry as possible."

* * *

Of course I deplore your tendency to dalliance with the demagogic muse. I hope you will not set your feet in the dirty paths — leading nowhither — of social and political "reform". . . . I hope you will not follow * * * in making a sale of your poet's birthright for a mess of "popularity." If you do I shall have to part company with you, as I have done with him and at least *one* of his betters, for I draw the line at demagogues and anarchists, however gifted and however beloved.

*"Dedication" poem to Ambrose Bierce.

Let the "poor" alone—they are oppressed by nobody but God. Nobody hates them, nobody despises. "The rich" love them a deal better than they love one another. But I'll not go into these matters; your own good sense must be your salvation if you are saved. I recognise the temptations of environment: you are of San Francisco, the paradise of ignorance, anarchy and general yellowness. Still, a poet is not altogether the creature of his place and time—at least not of his to-day and his parish.

By the way, you say that * * * is your only associate that knows anything of literature. She is a dear girl, but look out for her; she will make you an anarchist if she can, and persuade you to kill a President or two every fine morning. I warrant you she can pronounce the name of McKinley's assassin to the ultimate zed, and has a little graven image of him next her heart.

Yes, you can republish the Memorial Day poem without the *Post's* consent — could do so in "book form" even if the *Post* had copyrighted it, which it did not do. I think the courts have held that in purchasing work for publication in his newspaper or magazine the editor acquires no right in it, *except for that purpose*. Even if he copyright it that is only to protect him from other newspapers or magazines; the right to publish in a book remains with the author. Better ask a lawyer though — preferably without letting him know whether you are an editor or an author.

I ought to have answered (as well as able) these questions before, but I have been ill and worried, and have written few letters, and even done little work, and that only of the pot-boiling sort.

My daughter has recovered and returned to Los Angeles.

Please thank Miss * * * for the beautiful photographs —

I mean for being so beautiful as to "take" them, for doubt-less I owe their possession to you.

I wrote Doyle about you and he cordially praised your work as incomparably superior to his own and asked that you visit him. He's a lovable fellow and you'd not regret going to Santa Cruz and boozing with him.

Thank you for the picture of Grizzly and the cub of him.

Sincerely yours, with best regards to the pretty ever-so-much-better half of you,   AMBROSE BIERCE.

P. S. * * * * * * * * * * *

శ⊷ శ⊷ శ⊷

MY DEAR STERLING,

Where are you going to stop? — I mean at what stage of development? I presume you have not a "whole lot" of poems really writ, and have not been feeding them to me, the least good first, and not in the order of their produc-tion. So it must be that you are advancing at a stupendous rate. This last* beats any and all that went before — or I am bewitched and befuddled. I dare not trust myself to say what I think of it. In manner it is great, but the greatness of the theme! — that is beyond anything.

It is a new field, the broadest yet discovered. To para-phrase Coleridge,

You are the first that ever burst
Into that silent [unknown] sea—

a silent sea *because* no one else has burst into it in full song. True, there have been short incursions across the "border," but only by way of episode. The tremendous phenomena of Astronomy have never had adequate poetic treatment, their meaning adequate expression. You must make it your

*"The Testimony of the Suns."

The Olympia, Washington, D. C., March 15, 1902.

own domain. You shall be the poet of the skies, the prophet of the suns. Don't fiddle-faddle with such infinitesimal and tiresome trivialities as (for example) the immemorial squabbles of "rich" and "poor" on this "mote in the sun-beam." (Both "classes," when you come to that, are about equally disgusting and unworthy — there's not a pin's moral difference between them.) Let them cheat and pick pockets and cut throats to the satisfaction of their base instincts, but do thou regard them not. Moreover, by that great law of change which you so clearly discern, there can be no permanent composition of their nasty strife. "Settle" it how they will — another beat of the pendulum and all is as before; and ere another, Man will again be savage, sitting on his naked haunches and gnawing raw bones.

Yes, circumstances make the "rich" what they are. And circumstances make the poor what *they* are. I have known both, long and well. The rich — *while* rich — are a trifle better. There's nothing like poverty to nurture badness. But in this country there are no such "classes" as "rich" and "poor": as a rule, the wealthy man of to-day was a poor devil yesterday; the poor devils of to-day have an equal chance to be rich to-morrow — or would have if they had equal brains and providence. The system that gives them the chance is not an oppressive one. Under a really oppressive system a salesman in a village grocery could not have risen to a salary of one million dollars a year because he was worth it to his employers, as Schwab has done. True, some men get rich by dishonesty, but the poor commonly cheat as hard as they can and remain poor — thereby escaping observation and censure. The moral difference between cheating to the limit of a small opportunity and cheating to the limit of a great one is to me indiscernable.

The workman who "skimps his work" is just as much a rascal as the "director" who corners a crop.

As to "Socialism." I am something of a Socialist myself; that is, I think that the principle, which has always co-existed with competition, each safeguarding the other, may be advantageously extended. But those who rail against "the competitive system," and think they suffer from it, really suffer from their own unthrift and incapacity. For the competent and provident it is an ideally perfect system. As the other fellows are not of those who effect permanent reforms, or reforms of any kind, pure Socialism is the dream of a dream.

But why do I write all this. One's opinions on such matters are unaffected by reason and instance; they are born of feeling and temperament. There is a Socialist diathesis, as there is an Anarchist diathesis. Could you teach a bulldog to retrieve, or a sheep to fetch and carry? Could you make a "born artist" comprehend a syllogism? As easily persuade a poet that black is not whatever color he loves. Somebody has defined poetry as "glorious nonsense." It is not an altogether false definition, albeit I consider poetry the flower and fruit of speech and would rather write gloriously than sensibly. But if poets saw things as they are they would write no more poetry.

Nevertheless, I venture to ask you: *Can't* you see in the prosperity of the strong and the adversity of the weak a part of that great beneficent law, "the survival of the fittest"? Don't you see that such evils as inhere in "the competitive system" are evils only to individuals, but blessings to the race by gradually weeding out the incompetent and their progeny?

I've done, i' faith. Be any kind of 'ist or 'er that you will, but don't let it get into your ink. Nobody is calling you to deliver your land from Error's chain. What we want of you is poetry, not politics. And if you care for fame just have the goodness to consider if any "champion of the poor" has ever obtained it. From the earliest days down to Massanielo, Jack Cade and Eugene Debs the leaders and prophets of "the masses" have been held unworthy. And with reason too, however much injustice is mixed in with the right of it. Eventually the most conscientious, popular and successful "demagogue" comes into a heritage of infamy. The most brilliant gifts cannot save him. That will be the fate of Edwin Markham if he does not come out o' that, and it will be the fate of George Sterling if he will not be warned.

You think that "the main product of that system" (the "competitive") "is the love of money." What a case of the cart before the horse! The love of money is not the product, but the root, of the system — not the effect, but the cause. When one man desires to be better off than another he competes with him. You can abolish the system when you can abolish the desire — when you can make man as Nature did *not* make him, content to be as poor as the poorest. Do away with the desire to excel and you may set up your Socialism at once. But what kind of a race of sloths and slugs will you have?

But, bless me, I shall *never* have done if I say all that comes to me.

Why, of course my remarks about * * * were facetious — playful. She really is an anarchist, and her sympathies are with criminals, whom she considers the "product" of the laws, but — well, she inherited the diathesis and can no more help it than she can the color of her pretty eyes. But she is a child — and except in so far as her convictions make her impossible they do not count. She would not hurt a fly — not even if, like the toad, it had a precious jewel in its head that it did not work for. But I am speaking of the * * * that *I* knew. If I did not know that the anarchist leopard's spots "will wash," your words would make me think that she might have changed. It does not matter what women think, if thinking it may be called, and * * * will never be other than lovable.

Lest you have *not* a copy of the verses addressed to me I enclose one that I made myself. Of course their publication could not be otherwise than pleasing to me if you care to do it. You need not fear the "splendid weight" expression, and so forth — there is nothing "conceited" in the poem. As it was addressed to me, I have not criticised it — I *can't*. And I guess it needs no criticism.

I fear for the other two-thirds of this latest poem. If you descend from Arcturus to Earth, from your nebulae to your neighbors, from Life to lives, from the measureless immensities of space to the petty passions of us poor insects, won't you incur the peril of anti-climax? I doubt if you can touch the "human interest" after those high themes without an awful tumble. I should be sorry to see the poem "peter out," or "soak in." It would be as if Goethe had let his "Prologue in Heaven" expire in a coon song. You have reached the "heights of dream" all right, but how are you to stay there to the end? By the way, you must perfect yourself in Astronomy, or rather get a general knowledge of it, which I fear you lack. Be sure about the pronunciation of astronomical names.

I have read some of Jack London's work and think it clever. Of Whitaker I never before heard, I fear. If London wants to criticise your "Star poem" what's the objection? I should not think, though, from his eulogism of * * *, that he is very critical. * * *

Where are you to place Browning? Among thinkers. In his younger days, when he wrote in English, he stood among the poets. I remember writing once—of the thinker: "There's nothing more obscure than Browning except blacking." I'll stand to that.

No, don't take the trouble to send me a copy of these verses: I expect to see them in a book pretty soon. * * *

Sincerely yours, AMBROSE BIERCE.

❧ ❧ ❧

The Olympia,
Washington, D. C.,
March 31,
1902.

DEAR STERLING,

I am glad to know that you too have a good opinion of that poem.* One should know about one's own work. Most writers think their work good, but good writers know it. Pardon me if I underrated your astronomical knowledge. My belief was based on your use of those names. I never met with the spelling "Betelgeux"; and even if it is correct and picturesque I'd not use it if I were you, for it does not quite speak itself, and you can't afford to jolt the reader's attention from your thought to a matter of pronunciation. In my student days we, I am sure, were taught to say Procy′on. I don't think I've heard it pronounced since, and I've no authority at hand. If you are satisfied with Pro′cyon I suppose it is that. But your pronunciation was Aldeb′aran or your meter very crazy indeed. I asked (with an interrogation point) if it were not Aldeba′ran—and I think it is. Fomalhaut I don't know about; I thought it French and masculine. In that case it would, I suppose, be "ho," not "hote."

*"The Testimony of the Suns."

Don't cut out that stanza, even if "clime" doesn't seem to me to have anything to do with duration. The stanza is good enough to stand a blemish.

"Ye stand rebuked by suns who claim" — I was wrong in substituting "that" for "who," not observing that it would make it ambiguous. I merely yielded to a favorite impulse: to say "that" instead of "who," and did not count the cost.

Don't cut out *any* stanza — if you can't perfect them let them go imperfect.

"Without or genesis or end."

"Devoid of birth, devoid of end."

These are not so good as

"Without beginning, without end"; — I submit them to suggest a way to overcome that identical rhyme. All you have to do is get rid of the second "without." I should not like "impend."

Yes, I vote for Orion's *sword* of suns. "Cimetar" sounds better, but it is more specific — less generic. It is modern — or, rather, less ancient than "sword," and makes one think of Turkey and the Holy Land. But "sword" — there were swords before Homer. And I don't think the man who named this constellation ever saw a curved blade. And yet, and yet — "cimetar of suns" is "mighty catchin'."

No, indeed, I could not object to your considering the heavens in a state of war. I have sometimes fancied I could hear the rush and roar of it. Why, a few months ago I began a sonnet thus:

> "Not as two erring spheres together grind,
>   With monstrous ruin, in the vast of space,
>   Destruction born of that malign embrace —
>   Their hapless peoples all to death consigned — "etc.

I've been a star-gazer all my life — from my habit of being "out late," I guess; and the things have always seemed to me *alive*.

The change in the verses *ad meum*, from "*thy* clearer light" to "*the* clearer light" may have been made modestly or inadvertently — I don't recollect. It is, of course, no improvement and you may do as you please. I'm uniformly inadvertent, but intermittently modest.

* * *

A class of stuff that I can't (without "trouble in the office") write my own way I will not write at all. So I'm writing very little of anything but nonsense. * * *

With best regards to Mrs. Sterling and Miss Marian I am
Sincerely yours,
Ambrose Bierce.

Leigh died a year ago this morning. I wish I could stop counting the days.

♋ ♋ ♋

The Olympia, Washington, D. C., April 15, 1902.

Dear Sterling,

All right — I only wanted you to be *sure* about those names of stars; it would never do to be less than sure.

After all our talk (made by me) I guess that stanza would better stand as first written. "Clime"—climate—connotes temperature, weather, and so forth, in ordinary speech, but a poet may make his own definitions, I suppose, and compel the reader to study them out and accept them.

Your misgiving regarding your inability to reach so high a plane again as in this poem is amusing, but has an element of the pathetic. It certainly is a misfortune for a writer to do his *best* work early; but I fancy you'd better trust your genius and do its bidding whenever the monkey chooses to bite. "The Lord will provide." Of course you

have read Stockton's story "His Wife's Deceased Sister."
But Stockton gets on very well, despite "The Lady or the
Tiger." I've a notion that you'll find other tragedies among
the stars if earth doesn't supply you with high enough
themes.

Will I write a preface for the book? Why, yes, if you think
me competent. Emerson commands us to "hitch our wagon
to a star?" and, egad! here's a whole constellation — a universe — of stars to draw mine! It makes me blink to think
of it.

O yes, I'd like well enough to "leave the Journal," but —

Sincerely yours,

AMBROSE BIERCE.

❧ ❧ ❧

MY DEAR STERLING,

If rejection wounded, all writers would bleed at every pore. The Olympia,
Nevertheless, not my will but thine be done. Of course I Washington, D. C.,
shall be glad to go over your entire body of work again and 1902.
make suggestions if any occur to me. It will be no trouble —
I could not be more profitably employed than in critically
reading you, nor more agreeably.

* * *

Of course your star poem has one defect — if it is a defect — that limits the circle of understanding and admir-
ing readers — its lack of "*human* interest." We human
insects, as a rule, care for nothing but ourselves, and think
that is best which most closely touches such emotions and
sentiments as grow out of our relations, the one with
another. I don't share the preference, and a few others do
not, believing that there are things more interesting than
men and women. The Heavens, for example. But who
knows, or cares anything about them — even knows the

name of a single constellation? Hardly any one but the professional astronomers — and there are not enough of them to buy your books and give you fame. I should be sorry not to have that poem published — sorry if you did not write more of the kind. But while it may impress and dazzle "the many" it will not win them. They want you to finger their heart-strings and pull the cord that works their arms and legs. So you must finger and pull — too.

The Château Yquem came all right, and is good. Thank you for it — albeit I'm sorry you feel that you must do things like that. It is very conventional and, I fear, "proper." However, I remember that you used to do so when you could not by any stretch of imagination have felt that you were under an "obligation." So I guess it is all right — just your way of reminding me of the old days. Anyhow, the wine is so much better than my own that I've never a scruple when drinking it.

Has "Maid Marian" a photograph of me? — I don't remember. If not I'll send her one; I've just had some printed from a negative five or six years old. I've renounced the photograph habit, as one renounces other habits when age has made them ridiculous — or impossible.

Send me the typewritten book when you have it complete.

Sincerely yours,

AMBROSE BIERCE.

❧ ❧ ❧

Washington,
August 19,
1902.

MY DEAR STERLING,

I suppose you are in Seattle, but this letter will keep till your return.

I am delighted to know that I am to have "the book" so soon, and will give it my best attention and (if you still desire) some prefatory lines. Think out a good title and I shall myself be hospitable to any suggestion of my dæmon in the matter. He has given me nothing for the star poem yet.   * * *

You'll "learn in suffering what you teach in song," all right; but let us hope the song will be the richer for it. It *will* be. For that reason I never altogether "pity the sorrows" of a writer — knowing they are good for him. He needs them in his business. I suspect you must have shed a tear or two since I knew you.

I'm sending you a photograph, but you did not tell me if Maid Marian the Superb already has one — that's what I asked you, and if you don't answer I shall ask her.

* * *

Yes, I am fairly well, and, though not "happy," content. But I'm dreadfully sorry about Peterson.

Sincerely yours,
AMBROSE BIERCE.

I am about to break up my present establishment and don't know where my next will be. Better address me " Care N. Y. American and Journal Bureau, Washington, D. C."

You see I'm still chained to the oar of yellow journalism, but it is a rather light servitude.

֍ ֍ ֍

DEAR STERLING,

I fancy you must fear by this time that I did not get the poems, but I did. I'll get at them, doubtless, after awhile, though a good deal of manuscript — including a couple of novels! — is ahead of them; and one published book of bad poems awaits a particular condemnation.

Address me at 1321 Yale Street, Washington, D. C., December 20, 1902.

I'm a little embarrassed about the preface which I'm to write. I fear you must forego the preface or I the dedication. That kind of "coöperation" doesn't seem in very good taste: it smacks of "mutual admiration" in the bad sense, and the reviewers would probably call it "log-rolling." Of course it doesn't matter too much what the reviewers say, but it matters a lot what the intelligent readers think; and your book will have no others. I really shouldn't like to write the preface of a book dedicated to me, though I did not think of that at first.

The difficulty could be easily removed by *not* dedicating the book to me were it not that that would sacrifice the noble poem with my name atop of it. That poem is itself sufficiently dedicatory if printed by itself in the forepages of the book and labeled "Dedication — To Ambrose Bierce." I'm sure that vanity has nothing to do, or little to do, with my good opinion of the verses. And, after all, they *show* that I have said *to you* all that I could say to the reader in your praise and encouragement. What do you think?

As to dedicating individual poems to other fellows, I have not the slightest hesitancy in advising you against it. The practice smacks of the amateur and is never, I think, pleasing to anybody but the person so honored. The custom has fallen into "innocuous desuetude" and there appears to be no call for its revival. Pay off your obligations (if such there be) otherwise. You may put it this way if you like: The whole book being dedicated to me, no part of it *can* be dedicated to another. Or this way: Secure in my exalted position I don't purpose sharing the throne with rival (and inferior) claimants. They be gam doodled!

Seriously — but I guess it is serious enough as it stands. It occurs to me that in saying: "no part of it *can* be dedicated to another" I might be understood as meaning: "no part of it *must* be," etc. No; I mean only that the dedication to another would contradict the dedication to me. The two things are (as a matter of fact) incompatible.

Well, if you think a short preface by me preferable to the verses with my name, all right; I will cheerfully write it, and that will leave you free to honor your other friends if you care to. But those are great lines, and implying, as they do, all that a set preface could say, it seems to me that they ought to stand.

* * *

Maid Marian shall have the photograph.

Sincerely yours,

AMBROSE BIERCE.

ॐ ॐ ॐ

MY DEAR STERLING,

You are a brick. You shall do as you will. My chief reluctance is that if it become known, or *when* it becomes known, there may ensue a suspicion of my honesty in praising you and *your* book; for critics and readers are not likely to look into the matter of dates. For your sake I should be sorry to have it thought that my commendation was only a log-rolling incident; for myself, I should care nothing about it. This eel is accustomed to skinning.

1321 Yale Street, Washington, D. C., March 1, 1903.

It is not the least pleasing of my reflections that my friends have always liked my work — or me — well enough to want to publish my books at their own expense. Everything that I have written could go to the public that way if I would consent. In the two instances in which I did consent they got their money back all right, and I do not doubt that it will be so in this; for if I did not think there was at least a little profit in a book of mine I should not offer it to a publisher. "Shapes of Clay" *ought* to be published in

California, and it would have been long ago if I had not been so lazy and so indisposed to dicker with the publishers. Properly advertised — which no book of mine ever has been — it should sell there if nowhere else. Why, then, do *I* not put up the money? Well, for one reason, I've none to put up. Do you care for the other reasons?

But I must make this a condition. If there is a loss, *I* am to bear it. To that end I shall expect an exact accounting from your Mr. Wood, and the percentage that Scheff. purposes having him pay to me is to go to you. The copyright is to be mine, but nothing else until you are entirely recouped. But all this I will arrange with Scheff., who, I take it, is to attend to the business end of the matter, with, of course, your assent to the arrangements that he makes.

I shall write Scheff. to-day to go ahead and make his contract with Mr. Wood on these lines. Scheff. appears not to know who the "angel" in the case is, and he need not, unless, or until, you want him to.

I've a pretty letter from Maid Marian in acknowledgment of the photograph. I shall send one to Mrs. Sterling at once, in the sure and certain hope of getting another. It is good of her to remember my existence, considering that your scoundrelly monopoly of her permitted us to meet so seldom. I go in for a heavy tax on married men who live with their wives.

"She holds no truce with Death *or* Peace" means that with *one* of them she holds no truce; "nor" makes it mean that she holds no truce with *either*. The misuse of "or" (its use to mean "nor") is nearly everybody's upsetting sin. So common is it that "nor" instead usually sounds harsh.

I omitted the verses on "Puck," not because Bunner is dead, but because his work is dead too, and the verses

appear to lack intrinsic merit to stand alone. I shall perhaps omit a few more when I get the proofs (I wish you
could see the bushels I've left out already) and add a few
serious ones.

I'm glad no end that you and Scheff. have met. I'm fond
of the boy and he likes me, I think. He too has a book of
verses on the ways, and I hope for it a successful launching.
I've been through it all; some of it is great in the matter of
thews and brawn; some fine.

Pardon the typewriter; I wanted a copy of this letter.

Sincerely yours,
AMBROSE BIERCE.

᎒᎒ ᎒᎒ ᎒᎒

DEAR STERLING,

It is good to hear from you again and to know that the
book is so nearly complete as to be in the hands of the publishers. I dare say they will not have it, and you'll have to
get it out at your own expense. When it comes to that I
shall hope to be of service to you, as you have been to me.

The New York
"American" Bureau,
Washington, D. C.,
June 13,
1903.

So you like Scheff. Yes, he is a good boy and a good friend.
I wish you had met our friend Dr. Doyle, who has now
gone the long, lone journey. It has made a difference to me,
but that matters little, for the time is short in which to
grieve. I shall soon be going his way.

No, I shall not put anything about the * * * person into
"Shapes of Clay." His offence demands another kind of
punishment, and until I meet him he goes unpunished. I
once went to San Francisco to punish him (but that was in
hot blood) but * * * of "The Wave" told me the man was
a hopeless invalid, suffering from locomotor ataxia. I have
always believed that until I got your letter and one from
Scheff. Is it not so? — or *was* it not? If not he has good

reason to think me a coward, for his offence was what men are killed for; but of course one does not kill a helpless person, no matter what the offence is. If * * * lied to me I am most anxious to know it; he has always professed himself a devoted friend.

The passage that you quote from Jack London strikes me as good. I don't dislike the word "penetrate" — rather like it. It is in frequent use regarding exploration and discovery. But I think you right about "rippling"; it is too lively a word to be outfitted with such an adjective as "melancholy." I see London has an excellent article in "The Critic" on "The Terrible and Tragic in Fiction." He knows how to think a bit.

What do I think of Cowley-Brown and his "Goosequill"? I did not know that he had revived it; it died several years ago. I never met him, but in both Chicago and London (where he had "The Philistine," or "The Anti-Philistine," I do not at the moment remember which) he was most kind to me and my work. In one number of his magazine — the London one — he had four of my stories and a long article about me which called the blushes to my maiden cheek like the reflection of a red rose in the petal of a violet. Naturally I think well of Cowley-Brown.

You make me sad to think of the long leagues and the monstrous convexity of the earth separating me from your camp in the redwoods. There are few things that I would rather do than join that party; and I'd be the last to strike my tent and sling my swag. Alas, it cannot be — not this year. My outings are limited to short runs along this coast. I was about to set out on one this morning; and wrote a hasty note to Scheff in consequence of my preparations. In five hours I was suffering from asthma, and am now confined to my room. But for eight months of the year here I am immune — as I never was out there.

* * *

You will have to prepare yourself to endure a good deal of praise when that book is out. One does not mind when one gets accustomed to it. It neither pleases nor bores; you will have just no feeling about it at all. But if you really care for *my* praise I hope you have quoted a bit of it at the head of those dedicatory verses, as I suggested. That will give them a *raison d'être*.

With best regards to Mrs. Sterling and Katie I am sincerely yours, AMBROSE BIERCE.

P. S.—If not too much trouble you may remind Dick Partington and wife that I continue to exist and to remember them pleasantly.

❧ ❧ ❧

DEAR SCHEFF:

I got the proofs yesterday, and am returning them by this mail. The "report of progress" is every way satisfactory, and I don't doubt that a neat job is being done.

N. Y. "American" Bureau, Washington, D. C., [July, 1903].

The correction that you made is approved. I should have wanted and expected you to make many corrections and suggestions, but that I have had a purpose in making this book—namely, that it should represent my work at its average. In pursuance of this notion I was not hospitable even to suggestions, and have retained much work that I did not myself particularly approve; some of it trivial. You know I have always been addicted to trifling, and no book from which trivialities were excluded would fairly represent me.

I could not commend this notion in another. In your work and Sterling's I have striven hard to help you to come as near to perfection as we could, because perfection is what you and he want, and as young writers ought to want, the character of your work being higher than mine. I reached my literary level long ago, and seeing that it is not a high one there would seem to be a certain affectation, even a certain dishonesty, in making it seem higher than it is by republication of my best only. Of course I have not carried out this plan so consistently as to make the book dull: I had to "draw the line" at that.

I say all this because I don't want you and Sterling to think that I disdain assistance: I simply decided beforehand not to avail myself of its obvious advantages. You would have done as much for the book in one way as you have done in another.

I'll have to ask you to suggest that Mr. Wood have a man go over all the matter in the book, and see that none of the pieces are duplicated, as I fear they are. Reading the titles will not be enough: I might have given the same piece two titles. It will be necessary to compare first lines, I think. That will be drudgery which I'll not ask you to undertake: some of Wood's men, or some of the printer's men, will do it as well; it is in the line of their work.

The "Dies Irae" is the most earnest and sincere of religious poems; my travesty of it is mere solemn fooling, which fact is "given away" in the prose introduction, where I speak of my version being of possible service in the church! The travesty is not altogether unfair — it was inevitably suggested by the author's obvious inaccessibility to humor and logic — a peculiarity that is, however, observable in all religious literature, for it is a fundamental necessity to the religious mind. Without logic and a sense of the ludicrous a man is religious as certainly as without webbed feet a bird has the land habit.

It is funny, but I am a "whole lot" more interested in seeing your cover of the book than my contents of it. I don't at all doubt — since you dared undertake it — that your great conception will find a fit interpreter in your hand; so my feeling is not anxiety. It is just interest — pure interest in what is above my powers, but in which *you* can work. By the way, Keller, of the old "Wasp" was *not* the best of its cartoonists. The best — the best of *all* cartoonists if he had not died at eighteen — was another German, named Barkhaus. I have all his work and have long cherished a wish to republish it with the needed explanatory text — much of it being "local" and "transient." Some day, perhaps — most likely not. But Barkhaus was a giant.

How I envy you! There are few things that would please me so well as to "drop in" on you folks in Sterling's camp. Honestly, I think all that prevents is the (to me) killing journey by rail. And two months would be required, going and returning by sea. But the rail trip across the continent always gives me a horrible case of asthma, which lasts for weeks. I shall never take *that* journey again if I can avoid it. What times you and they will have about the campfire and the table! I feel like an exile, though I fear I don't look and act the part.

I did not make the little excursion I was about to take when I wrote you recently. Almost as I posted the letter I was taken ill and have not been well since.

Poor Doyle! how thoughtful of him to provide for the destruction of my letters! But I fear Mrs. Doyle found some of them queer reading — if she read them.

* * *

Great Scott! if ever they begin to publish mine there will be a circus! For of course the women will be the chief sinners, and — well, they have material a-plenty; they can make many volumes, and your poor dead friend will have so bad a reputation that you'll swear you never knew him. I dare say, though, you have sometimes been indiscreet, too. *My* besetting sin has been in writing to my girl friends as if they were sweethearts — the which they'll doubtless not be slow to affirm. The fact that they write to me in the same way will be no defense; for when I'm worm's meat I can't present the proof — and wouldn't if I could. Maybe it won't matter — if I don't turn in my grave and so bother the worms.

As Doyle's "literary executor" I fear your duties will be light: he probably did not leave much manuscript. I judge from his letters that he was despondent about his work and the narrow acceptance that it had. So I assume that he did not leave much more than the book of poems, which no publisher would (or will) take.

You are about to encounter the same stupid indifference of the public — so is Sterling. I'm sure of Sterling, but don't quite know how it will affect *you*. You're a pretty sturdy fellow, physically and mentally, but this *may* hurt horribly. I pray that it do not, and could give you — perhaps have given you — a thousand reasons why it *should* not. You are still young and your fame may come while you live; but you must not expect it now, and doubtless do not. To me, and I hope to you, the approval of one person who knows is sweeter than the acclaim of ten thousand who do not — whose acclaim, indeed, I would rather not have. If you do not *feel* this in every fibre of your brain and heart, try to learn to feel it — practice feeling it, as one practices some athletic feat necessary to health and strength.

Thank you very much for the photograph. You are growing too infernally handsome to be permitted to go about unchained. If I had your "advantages" of youth and comeliness I'd go to the sheriff and ask him to lock me up. That would be the honorable thing for you to do, if you don't mind. God be with you — but inattentive.

AMBROSE BIERCE.

ॐ ॐ ॐ

DEAR STERLING,

I fear that among the various cares incident to my departure from Washington I forgot, or neglected, to acknowledge the Joaquin Miller book that you kindly sent me. I was glad to have it. It has all his characteristic merits and demerits—among the latter, his interminable prolixity, the thinness of the thought, his endless repetition of favorite words and phrases, many of them from his other poems, his mispronunciation, his occasional flashes of prose, and so forth.

Aurora, Preston Co., West Virginia, August 15, 1903.

Scheff tells me his book is out and mine nearly out. But what of yours? I do fear me it never will be out if you rely upon its "acceptance" by any American publisher. If it meets with no favor among the publisher tribe we must nevertheless get it out; and you will of course let me do what I can. That is only tit for tat. But tell me about it.

I dare say Scheff, who is clever at getting letters out of me — the scamp! — has told you of my being up here atop of the Alleghenies, and why I *am* here. I'm having a rather good time. * * * Can you fancy me playing croquet, cards, lawn — no, thank God, I've escaped lawn tennis and golf! In respect of other things, though, I'm a glittering specimen of the Summer Old Man.

Did *you* have a good time in the redwoods?

Please present my compliments to Madame (and Mademoiselle) Sterling. Sincerely yours,   AMBROSE BIERCE.

DEAR STERLING,

I return the verses with a few suggestions.

I'm sorry your time for poetry is so brief. But take your pencil and figure out how much you would write in thirty years (I hope you'll live that long) at, say, six lines a day. You'll be surprised by the result — and encouraged. Remember that 50,000 words make a fairly long book.

You make me shudder when you say you are reading the "Prattle" of years. I haven't it and should hardly dare to read it if I had. There is so much in it to deplore — so much that is not wise — so much that was the expression of a mood or a whim — so much was not altogether sincere — so many half-truths, and so forth. Make allowances, I beg, and where you cannot, just forgive.

Scheff has mentioned his great desire that you join the Bohemian Club. I know he wants me to advise you to do so. So I'm between two fires and would rather not advise at all. There are advantages (obvious enough) in belonging; and to one of your age and well grounded in sobriety and self-restraint generally, the disadvantages are not so great as to a youngster like Scheff. (Of course he is not so young as he seems to me; but he is younger by a few years and a whole lot of thought than you.)

The trouble with that kind of club — with any club — is the temptation to waste of time and money; and the danger of the drink habit. If one is proof against these a club is all right. I belong to one myself in Washington, and at one time came pretty near to "running" it.

* * *

No, I don't think Scheff's view of Kipling just. He asked me about putting that skit in the book. It *was* his view and, that being so, I could see no reason for suppressing it in deference to those who do not hold it. I like free speech, though I'd not accord it to my enemies if I were Dictator. I should not think it for the good of the State to let * * * write verses, for example. The modern fad Tolerance does not charm me, but since it is all the go I'm willing that my friends should have their fling.

I dare say Scheff is unconscious of Kipling's paternity in the fine line in "Back, back to Nature":

"Loudly to the shore cries the surf upon the sea."

But turn to "The Last Chanty," in "The Seven Seas," fill your ears with it and you'll write just such a line yourself.

* * *

God be decent to you, old man.

AMBROSE BIERCE.

DEAR STERLING,

I have yours of the 5th. Before now you have mine of *some* date. * * *

Aurora, West Virginia, September 12, 1903.

I'm glad you like London; I've heard he is a fine fellow and have read one of his books — "The Son of the Wolf," I think is the title — and it seemed clever work mostly. The general impression that remains with me is that it is always winter and always night in Alaska.

* * *

* * * will probably be glad to sell his scrap-book later, to get bread. He can't make a living out of the labor unions alone. I wish he were not a demgagoue and would not, as poor Doyle put it, go a-whoring after their Muse. When he returns to truth and poetry I'll receive him back into favor and he may kick me if he wants to.

No, I can't tell you how to get "Prattle"; if I could I'd

not be without it myself. You ask me when I began it in the "Examiner." Soon after Hearst got the paper — I don't know the date — they can tell you at the office and will show you the bound volumes.

I have the bound volumes of the "Argonaut" and "Wasp" during the years when I was connected with them, but my work in the "Examiner" (and previously in the "News Letter" and the London "Fun" and "Figaro" and other papers) I kept only in a haphazard and imperfect way.

I don't recollect giving Scheff any "epigram" on woman or anything else. So I can't send it to you. I amuse myself occasionally with that sort of thing in the "Journal" ("American") and suppose Hearst's other papers copy them, but the "environment" is uncongenial and uninspiring.

Do I think extracts from "Prattle" would sell? I don't think anything of mine will sell. I could make a dozen books of the stuff that I have "saved up" — have a few ready for publication now — but all is vanity so far as profitable publication is concerned. Publishers want nothing from me but novels — and I'll die first.

Who is * * * — and why? It is good of London to defend me against him. I fancy all you fellows have a-plenty of defending me to do, though truly it is hardly worth while. All my life I have been hated and slandered by all manner of persons except good and intelligent ones; and I don't greatly mind. I knew in the beginning what I had to expect, and I know now that, like spanking, it hurts (sometimes) but does not harm. And the same malevolence that has surrounded my life will surround my memory if I am remembered. Just run over in your mind the names of men who have told the truth about their unworthy fellows and about human nature "as it was given them to see it." They are the bogie-men of history. None of them has escaped vilification. Can poor little I hope for anything better? When you strike you are struck. The world is a skunk, but it has rights; among them that of retaliation. Yes, you deceive yourself if you think the little fellows of letters "like" you, or rather if you think they will like you when they know how big you are. They will lie awake nights to invent new lies about you and new means of spreading them without detection. But you have your revenge: in a few years they'll all be dead — just the same as if you had killed them. Better yet, you'll be dead yourself. So — you have my entire philosophy in two words: "Nothing matters."

Reverting to Scheff. What he has to fear (if he cares) is not incompetent criticism, but public indifference. That does not bite, but poets are an ambitious folk and like the limelight and the center of the stage. Maybe Scheff is different, as I know you are. Try to make him so if he isn't. * * * Wise poets write for one another. If the public happens to take notice, well and good. Sometimes it does — and then the wise poet would a blacksmith be. But this screed is becoming an essay.

Please give my love to all good Sterlings — those by birth and those by marriage. * * *

My friends have returned to Washington, and I'm having great times climbing peaks (they are knobs) and exploring gulches and cañons — for which these people have no names — poor things. My dreamland is still unrevisited. They found a Confederate soldier over there the other day, with his rifle alongside. I'm going over to beg his pardon.

Ever yours,
AMBROSE BIERCE.

Washington, D. C.
[Postmarked
October 12,
1903.]

My dear Sterling,

I have Jack London's books — the one from you and the one from him. I thank you and shall find the time to read them. I've been back but a few days and find a brace of dozen of books "intitualed" "Shapes of Clay." That the splendid work done by Scheff and Wood and your other associates in your labor of love is most gratifying to me should "go without saying." Surely *I* am most fortunate in having so good friends to care for my interests. Still, there will be an aching void in the heart of me until *your* book is in evidence. Honest, I feel more satisfaction in the work of you and Scheff than in my own. It is through you two that I expect my best fame. And how generously you accord it! — unlike certain others of my "pupils," whom I have assisted far more than I did you.

My trip through the mountains has done my health good — and my heart too. It was a "sentimental journey" in a different sense from Sterne's. Do you know, George, the charm of a new emotion? Of course you do, but at my age I had thought it impossible. Well, I had it repeatedly. Bedad, I think of going again into my old "theatre of war," and setting up a cabin there and living the few days that remain to me in meditation and sentimentalizing. But I should like you to be near enough to come up some Saturday night with some'at to drink. Sincerely yours,

AMBROSE BIERCE.

৵ ৵ ৵

N. Y. Journal Office,
Washington, D. C.,
October 21,
1903.

My dear Sterling,

I'm indebted to you for two letters — awfully good ones. In the last you tell me that your health is better, and I can see for myself that your spirits are. This you attribute to exercise, correctly, no doubt. You need a lot of the open air — we all do. I can give myself hypochondria in forty-eight hours by staying in-doors. The sedentary life and abstracted contemplation of one's own navel are good for Oriental gods only. We spirits of a purer fire need sunlight and the hills. My own recent wanderings afoot and horse-back in the mountains did me more good than a sermon. And you have "the hills back of Oakland"! God, what would I not give to help you range them, the dear old things! Why, I know every square foot of them from Walnut Creek to Niles Cañon. Of course they swarm with ghosts, as do all places out there, even the streets of San Francisco; but I and my ghosts always get on well together. With the female ones my relations are sometimes a bit better than they were with the dear creatures when they lived.

I guess I did not acknowledge the splendidly bound "Shapes" that you kindly sent, nor the Jack London books. Much thanks.

I'm pleased to know that Wood expects to sell the whole edition of my book, but am myself not confident of that.

So we are to have your book soon. Good, but I don't like your indifference to its outward and visible aspect. Some of my own books have offended, and continue to offend, in that way. At best a book is not too beautiful; at worst it is hideous. Be advised a bit by Scheff in this matter; his taste seems to me admirable and I'm well pleased by his work on the "Shapes"; even his covers, which I'm sorry to learn do not please Wood, appear to me excellent. I approved the design before he executed it — in fact chose it from several that he submitted. Its only fault seems to me too much gold leaf, but that is a fault "on the right side." In that and all the rest of the work (except my own) experts here are delighted. I gave him an absolutely free hand

and am glad I did. I don't like the ragged leaves, but he does not either, on second thought. The public — the reading public — I fear does, just now.

I'll get at your new verses in a few days. It will be, as always it is, a pleasure to go over them.

About "Prattle." I should think you might get help in that matter from Oscar T. Schuck, 2916 Laguna St. He used to suffer from "Prattle" a good deal, but is very friendly, and the obtaining it would be in the line of his present business.

How did you happen to hit on Markham's greatest two lines — but I need not ask that — from "The Wharf of Dreams"?

Well, I wish I could think that those lines of mine in "Geotheos" were worthy to be mentioned with Keats "magic casements" and Coleridge's "woman wailing for her demon lover." But I don't think any lines of anybody are. I laugh at myself to remember that Geotheos, never before in print I believe, was written for E. L. G. Steele to read before a "young ladies' seminary" somewhere in the cow counties! Like a man of sense he didn't read it. I don't share your regret that I have not devoted myself to serious poetry. I don't think of myself as a poet, but as a satirist; so I'm entitled to credit for what little gold there may be in the mud I throw. But if I professed gold-throwing, the mud which I should surely mix with the missiles would count against me. Besides, I've a preference for being the first man in a village, rather than the second man in Rome. Poetry is a ladder on which there is now no room at the top — unless you and Scheff throw down some of the chaps occupying the upper rung. It looks as if you might, but I could not. When old Homer, Shakspeare and that crowd —

building better than Ozymandias — say: "Look on my works, ye mighty, and despair!" I, considering myself specially addressed, despair. The challenge of the wits does not alarm me.

* * *

As to your problems in grammar.

If you say: "There is no hope *or* fear" you say that *one* of them does not exist. In saying: "There is no hope *nor* fear" you say that *both* do not exist — which is what you mean.

"Not to weary you, I shall say that I fetched the book from his cabin." Whether that is preferable to "I will say" depends on just what is meant; both are grammatical. The "shall" merely indicates an intention to say; the "will" implies a certain shade of concession in saying it.

It is no trouble to answer such questions, *nor* to do anything else to please you. I only hope I make it clear.

I don't know if all my "Journal" work gets into the "Examiner," for I don't see all the issues of either paper. I'm not writing much anyhow. They don't seem to want much from me, and their weekly check is about all that I want from them.

* * *

No, I don't know any better poem of Kipling than "The Last Chanty." Did you see what stuff of his Prof. Harry Thurston Peck, the Hearst outfit's special literary censor, chose for a particular commendation the other day? Yet Peck is a scholar, a professor of Latin and a writer of merited distinction. Excepting the ability to write poetry, the ability to understand it is, I think, the rarest of intellectual gifts. Let us thank "whatever gods may be" that we have it, if we haven't so very much else.

I've a lovely birch stick a-seasoning for you — cut it up in the Alleghanies.   * * *

Sincerely yours,

AMBROSE BIERCE.

Washington, D. C., October 29, 1903. DEAR GEORGE,

I return the verses — with apology for tardiness. I've been "full up" with cares.   * * *

I would not change "Religion" to "Dogma" (if I were you) for all "the pious monks of St. Bernard." Once you begin to make concessions to the feelings of this person or that there is no place to stop and you may as well hang up the lyre. Besides, Dogma does not "seek"; it just impudently declares something to have been found. However, it is a small matter — nothing can destroy the excellence of the verses. I only want to warn you against yielding to a temptation which will assail you all your life — the temptation to "edit" your thought for somebody whom it may pain. Be true to Truth and let all stand from under.

Yes, I think the quatrain that you wrote in Col. Eng's book good enough to go in your own. But I'd keep "discerning," instead of substituting "revering." In art discernment *carries* reverence.

Of course I expect to say something of Scheff's book, but in no paper with which I have a present connection can I regularly "review" it. Hearst's papers would give it incomparably the widest publicity, but they don't want "reviews" from me. They have Millard, who has already reviewed it — right well too — and Prof. Peck — who possibly might review it if it were sent to him. "Prof. Harry Thurston Peck, care of 'The American,' New York City." Mention it to Scheff. I'm trying to find out what I can do.

I'm greatly pleased to observe your ability to estimate the relative value of your own poems — a rare faculty. "To Imagination" is, *I* think, the best of all your short ones.

I'm impatient for the book. It, too, I shall hope to write something about. Sincerely yours,   AMBROSE BIERCE.

⁂ ⁂ ⁂

DEAR GEORGE,

A thousand cares have prevented my writing to you — and Scheff. And this is to be a "busy day." But I want to say that I've not been unmindful of your kindness in sending the book — which has hardly left my pocket since I got it. And I've read nothing in it more than once, excepting the "Testimony." *That* I've studied, line by line — and "precept by precept" — finding in it always "something rich and strange." It is greater than I knew; it is the greatest "ever"!

Navarre Hotel and Importation Co., Seventh Avenue and 38th St., New York, December 26, 1903.

I'm saying a few words about it in tomorrow's "American" — would that I had a better place for what I say and more freedom of saying. But they don't want, and won't have, "book reviews" from me; probably because I will not undertake to assist their advertising publishers. So I have to disguise my remarks and work up to them as parts of another topic. In this case I have availed myself of my favorite "horrible example," Jim Riley, who ought to be proud to be mentioned on the same page with you. After all, the remarks may not appear; I have the *littlest* editor that ever blue-penciled whatever he thought particularly dear to the writer. I'm here for only a few days, I hope.

* * *

I want to say that you seem to me greatest when you have the greatest subject — not flowers, women and all that, — but something above the flower-and-woman belt —

something that you see from altitudes from which *they* are unseen and unsmelled. Your poetry is incomparable with that of our other poets, but your thought, philosophy, — that is greater yet. But I'm writing this at a desk in the reading room of a hotel; when I get home I'll write you again.

I'm concerned about your health, of which I get bad reports. Can't you go to the mesas of New Mexico and round up cattle for a year or two — or do anything that will permit, or compel, you to sleep out-of-doors under your favorite stars — something that will *not* permit you to enter a house for even ten minutes? You say no. Well, some day you'll *have* to — when it is too late — like Peterson, my friend Charley Kaufman and so many others, who might be living if they had gone into that country in time and been willing to make the sacrifice when it would have done good. You can go *now* as well as *then*; and if now you'll come back well, if then, you'll not only sacrifice your salary, "prospects," and so forth, but lose your life as well. I *know* that kind of life would cure you. I've talked with dozens of men whom it did cure.

· You'll die of consumption if you don't. Twenty-odd years ago I was writing articles on the out-of-doors treatment for consumption. Now — only just now — the physicians are doing the same, and establishing out-of-door sanitaria for consumption.

You'll say you haven't consumption. I don't say that you have. But you will have if you listen to yourself saying: "I can't do it." * * *

Pardon me, my friend, for this rough advice as to your personal affairs: I am greatly concerned about you. Your life is precious to me and to the world. Sincerely yours,

AMBROSE BIERCE.

My dear George,

Thank you so much for the books and the inscription — Washington, D. C., January 8, 1904. which (as do all other words of praise) affects me with a sad sense of my shortcomings as writer and man. Things of that kind from too partial friends point out to me with a disquieting significance what I ought to be; and the contrast with what I am hurts. Maybe you feel enough that way sometimes to understand. You are still young enough to profit by the pain; *my* character is made — *my* opportunities are gone. But it does not greatly matter — nothing does. I have some little testimony from you and Scheff and others that I have not lived altogether in vain, and I know that I have greater satisfaction in my slight connection with your and their work than in my own. Also a better claim to the attention and consideration of my fellow-men.

Never mind about the "slow sale" of my book; I did not expect it to be otherwise, and my only regret grows out of the fear that some one may lose money by the venture. *It is not to be you.* You know I am still a little "in the dark" as to what *you* have really done in the matter. I wish you would tell me if any of your own money went into it. The contract with Wood is all right; it was drawn according to my instructions and I shall not even accept the small royalty allowed me if anybody is to be "out." If *you* are to be out I shall not only not accept the royalty, but shall reimburse you to the last cent. Do you mind telling me about all that? In any case don't "buy out Wood" and don't pay out anything for advertising nor for anything else.

The silence of the reviewers does not trouble me, any more than it would you. Their praise of my other books never, apparently, did me any good. No book published in this country ever received higher praise from higher sources than my first collection of yarns. But the book was never a "seller," and doubtless never will be. That *I* like it fairly well is enough. You and I do not write books to sell; we write — or rather publish — just because we like to. We've no right to expect a profit from fun.

It is odd and amusing that you could have supposed that I had any other reason for not writing to you than a fixed habit of procrastination, some preoccupation with my small affairs and a very burdensome correspondence. Probably you *could* give me a grievance by trying hard, but if you ever are conscious of not having tried you may be sure that I haven't the grievance.

I should have supposed that the author of "Viverols" and several excellent monographs on fish would have understood your poems. (O no; I don't mean that your Muse is a mermaid.) Perhaps he did, but you know how temperate of words men of science are by habit. Did you send a book to Garrett Serviss? I should like to know what he thinks of the "Testimony." As to Joaquin, it is his detestable habit, as it was Longfellow's, to praise all poetry submitted to him, and he said of Madge Morris's coyote poem the identical thing that he says of your work. Sorry to disillusionize you, but it is so.

As to your health. You give me great comfort.* * * But it was not only from Scheff that I had bad accounts of you and "your cough." Scheff, indeed, has been reticent in the matter, but evidently anxious; and you yourself have written despondently and "forecasted" an early passing away. If nothing is the matter with you and your lungs some of your friends are poor observers. I'm happy to have your testimony, and beg to withdraw my project for your recovery. You whet my appetite for that new poem. The lines

> "The blue-eyed vampire, sated at her feast,
> Smiles bloodily against the leprous moon"

give me the shivers. Gee! they're awful! Sincerely yours,

AMBROSE BIERCE.

ఎంఎం ఎం

DEAR GEORGE,

* * *

You should not be irritated by the "conspiracy of silence" Washington, D. C., February 5, 1904. about me on the part of the "Call," the "Argonaut" and other papers. Really my enemies are under no obligation to return good for evil; I fear I should not respect them if they did. * * *, his head still sore from my many beatings of that "distracted globe," would be a comic figure stammering his sense of my merit and directing attention to the excellence of the literary wares on my shelf.

As to the pig of a public, its indifference to a diet of pearls — *our* pearls — was not unknown to me, and truly it does not trouble me anywhere except in the pocket. *That* pig, too, is not much beholden to me, who have pounded the snout of it all my life. Why should it assist in the rite? Its indifference to *your* work constitutes a new provocation and calls for added whacks, but not its indifference to mine.

The Ashton Stevens interview was charming. His finding you and Scheff together seems too idyllic to be true — I thought it a fake. He put in quite enough — too much — about me. As to Joaquin's hack at me — why, that was magnanimity itself in one who, like most of us, does not offset blame against praise, subtract the latter from the former and find matter for thanks in the remainder. You know "what fools we mortals be"; criticism that is not all honey is all vinegar. Nobody has more delighted than I in pointing out the greatness of Joaquin's great work; but nobody than I has more austerely condemned * * *, his vanity and the general humbugery that makes his prose so insupportable. Joaquin is a good fellow, all the same, and you should not demand of him impossible virtues and a reach of reasonableness that is alien to him.

* * *

I have the books you kindly sent and have planted two or three in what I think fertile soil which I hope will produce a small crop of appreciation.

* * *

And the poem!* I hardly know how to speak of it. No poem in English of equal length has so bewildering a wealth of imagination. Not Spenser himself has flung such a profusion of jewels into so small a casket. Why, man, it takes away the breath! I've read and reread — read it for the expression and read it for the thought (always when I speak of the "thought" in your work I mean the meaning — which is another thing) and I shall read it many times more. And pretty soon I'll get at it with my red ink and see if I can suggest anything worth your attention. I fear not.

* * *

Sincerely yours,

Ambrose Bierce.

ॐ ॐ ॐ

"New York American" Office, Washington, D. C., February 29, 1904.

Dear George,

I wrote you yesterday. Since then I have been rereading your letter. I wish you would not say so much about what I have done for you, and how much it was worth to you, and all that. I should be sorry to think that I did not do a little for you — I tried to. But, my boy, you should know that I don't keep that kind of service *on sale*. Moreover, I'm

*"A Wine of Wizardry."

amply repaid by what *you* have done for *me* — I mean with your pen. Do you suppose *I* do not value such things? Does it seem reasonable to think me unpleasured by those magnificent dedicatory verses in your book? Is it nothing to me to be called "Master" by such as you? Is my nature so cold that I have no pride in such a pupil? There is no obligation in the matter — certainly none that can be suffered to satisfy itself out of your pocket.

You greatly overestimate the sums I spend in "charity." I sometimes help some poor devil of an unfortunate over the rough places, but not to the extent that you seem to suppose. I couldn't — I've too many regular, constant, *legitimate* demands on me. Those, mostly, are what keep me poor.

* * *

Maybe you think it odd that I've not said a word in print about any of your work except the "Testimony." It is not that I don't appreciate the minor poems — I do. But I don't like to scatter; I prefer to hammer on a single nail — to push one button until someone hears the bell. When the "Wine" is published I'll have another poem that is not only great, but striking — notable — to work on. However good, or even great, a short poem with such a title as "Poesy," "Music," "To a Lily," "A White Rose," and so forth, cannot be got into public attention. Some longer and more notable work, of the grander manner, may *carry* it, but of itself it will not go. Even a bookful of its kind will not. Not till you're famous.

Your letter regarding your brother (who has not turned up) was needless — I could be of no assistance in procuring him employment. I've tried so often to procure it for others, and so vainly, that nobody could persuade me to try any more. I'm not fond of the character of suppliant, nor of being "turned down" by the little men who run this Government. Of course I'm not in favor with this Administration, not only because of my connection with Democratic newspapers, but because, also, I sometimes venture to dissent openly from the doctrine of the divinity of those in high station — particularly Teddy.

I'm sorry you find your place in the office intolerable. That is "the common lot of all" who work for others. I have chafed under the yoke for many years — a heavier yoke, I think, than yours. It does not fit my neck anywhere. Some day perhaps you and I will live on adjoining ranches in the mountains — or in adjoining caves — "the world forgetting, by the world forgot." I have really been on the point of hermitizing lately, but I guess I'll have to continue to live like a reasonable human being a little longer until I can release myself with a conscience void of offense to my creditors and dependents. But "the call of the wild" sounds, even in my dreams.

You ask me if you should write in "A Wine of Wizardry" vein, or in that of "The Testimony of the Suns." Both. I don't know in which you have succeeded the better. And I don't know anyone who has succeeded better in either. To succeed in both is a marvelous performance. You may say that the one is fancy, the other imagination, which is true, but not the whole truth. The "Wine" has as true imagination as the other, and fancy into the bargain. I like your grandiose manner, and I like the other as well. In terms of another art I may say — rear great towers and domes. Carve, also, friezes. But I'd not bother to cut single finials and small decorations. However exquisite the workmanship, they are not worth your present attention. If you were a painter (as, considering your wonderful sense of color, you doubtless could have been) your large canvases would be your best.   * * *

I don't care if that satire of Josephare refers to me or not; it was good. He may jump on me if he wants to — I don't mind. All I ask is that he do it well.

* * *

I passed yesterday with Percival Pollard, viewing the burnt district of Baltimore. He's a queer duck whom I like, and he likes your work. I'm sending you a copy of "The Papyrus," with his "rehabilitation" of the odious Oscar Wilde. Wilde's work is all right, but what can one do with the work of one whose name one cannot speak before women?   * * *

Sincerely yours,
AMBROSE BIERCE.

DEAR GEORGE,

The "belatedness" of your letter only made *me* fear that *I* had offended *you*. Odd that we should have such views of each other's sensitiveness. Washington, D. C., April 19, 1904.

About Wood. No doubt that he is doing all that he can, but — well, he is not a publisher. For example: He sent forty or fifty "Shapes" here. They lie behind a counter at the bookseller's — not even *on* the counter. There are probably not a dozen persons of my acquaintance in Washington who know that I ever wrote a book. Now *how* are even these to know about *that* book? The bookseller does not advertise the books he has on sale and the public does not go rummaging behind his counters. A publisher's methods are a bit different, naturally.

Only for your interest I should not care if my books sold or not; they exist and will not be destroyed; every book will eventually get to *somebody*.

* * *

It seems to be a matter for you to determine — whether Wood continues to try to sell the book or it is put in other hands if he is ever tired of it. Remember, I don't care a rap what happens to the book except as a means of reimbursing you; I want no money and I want no glory. If you and Wood can agree, do in all things as you please.

I return Wood's letters; they show what I knew before: that the public and the librarians would not buy that book. Let us discuss this matter no more, but at some time in the future you tell me how much you are out of pocket.

Your book shows that a fellow can get a good deal of glory with very little profit. You are now famous — at least on the Pacific Coast; but I fancy you are not any "for'arder" in the matter of wealth than you were before. I too have some reputation—a little wider, as yet, than yours. Well, my work sells tremendously — in Mr. Hearst's newspapers, at the price of a small fraction of one cent! Offered by itself, in one-dollar and two-dollar lots, it tempts nobody to fall over his own feet in the rush to buy. A great trade, this of ours!

I note with interest the "notices" you send. The one by Monahan is amusing with its gabble about your "science." To most men, as to him, a mention of the stars suggests astronomy, with its telescopes, spectroscopes and so forth. Therefore it is "scientific." To tell such men that there is nothing of science in your poem would puzzle them greatly.

I don't think poor Lang meant to do anything but his best and honestest. He is a rather clever and rather small fellow and not to be blamed for the limitations of his in-

sight. I have repeatedly pointed out in print that it requires
genius to discern genius at first hand. Lang has written
almost the best, if not quite the best, sonnet in the language — yet he is no genius.

* * *

Why, of course — why should you not help the poor devil,
* * *; I used to help him myself — introduced him to the
public and labored to instruct him. Then — but it is unspeakable and so is he. He will bite your hand if you feed
him, but I think I'd throw a crust to him myself.

* * *

No, I don't agree with you about Homer, nor "stand for"
your implied view that narrative poetry is not "pure
poetry." Poetry seems to me to speak with a thousand
voices — "a various language." The miners have a saying:
"Gold is where you find it." So is poetry; I'm expecting to
find it some fine day in the price list of a grocery store. I
fancy *you* could put it there.

* * *

As to Goethe, the more you read him, the better you
will love Heine.

Thank you for "A Wine of Wizardry" — amended. It
seems to me that the fake dictum of "Merlin-sage" (I don't
quite perceive the necessity of the hyphen) is better than
the hackneyed Scriptural quotation. It is odd, but my
recollection is that it was the "sick enchantress" who cried
"unto Betelgeuse a mystic word." Was it not so in the copy
that I first had, or do I think so merely because the cry of
one is more lone and awful than the cry of a number?

I am still of the belief that the poem should have at least
a few breaks in it, for I find myself as well as the public
more or less — I, doubtless, less than the public — indis-

posed to tackle solid columns of either verse or prose. I told you this poem "took away one's breath," — give a fellow, can't you, a chance to recover it now and again.

"Space to breathe, how short soever."

Nevertheless, not my will but thine be done, on earth as it is in San Francisco. Sincerely yours, Ambrose Bierce.

❧ ❧ ❧

Dear George,

To begin at the beginning, I shall of course be pleased to meet Josephare if he come this way; if only to try to solve the problem of what is in a fellow who started so badly and in so short a time was running well, with a prospect of winning "a place." Byron, you know, was the same way and Tennyson not so different. Still their start was not so bad as Josephare's. I freely confess that I thought him a fool. It is "one on me."

* * *

I wonder if a London house would publish "Shapes of Clay." Occasionally a little discussion about me breaks out in the London press, blazes up for a little while and "goes up in smoke." I enclose some evidences of the latest one — which you may return if you remember to do so. The letter of "a deeply disappointed man" was one of rollicking humor suggested by some articles of Barr about me and a private intimation from him that I should publish some more books in London.

Yes, I've dropped "The Passing Show" again, for the same old reason — wouldn't stand the censorship of my editor. I'm writing for the daily issues of The American, mainly, and, as a rule, anonymously. It's "dead easy" work.   * * *

It is all right — that "cry unto Betelgeuse"; the "sick en-chantress" passage is good enough without it. I like the added lines of the poem. Here's another criticism: The "Without" and "Within," beginning the first and third lines, respectively, *seem* to be antithetic, when they are not, the latter having the sense of "into," which I think might, for clearness, be substituted for it without a displeasing break of the metre — a trochee for an iambus.

Why should I not try "The Atlantic" with this poem? — if you have not already done so. I could write a brief note about it, saying what *you* could not say, and possibly win-ning attention to the work. If you say so I will. It is impos-sible to imagine a magazine editor rejecting that amazing poem. I have read it at least twenty times with ever in-creasing admiration.

Your book, by the way, is still my constant companion — I carry it in my pocket and read it over and over, in the street cars and everywhere. *All* the poems are good, though the "Testimony" and "Memorial Day" are supreme — the one in grandeur, the other in feeling.

I send you a criticism in a manuscript letter from a friend who complains of your "obscurity," as many have the can-dor to do. It requires candor to do that, for the fault is in the critic's understanding. Still, one who understands Shak-speare and Milton is not without standing as a complain-ing witness in the court of literature.

* * *

My favorite translation of Homer is that of Pope, of whom it is the present fashion to speak disparagingly, as it is of Byron. I know all that can be said against them, and say *some* of it myself, but I wish their detractors had a little of their brains. I know too that Pope's translations of The

Iliad and The Odyssey are rather paraphrases than translations. But I love them just the same, while wondering
(with you, doubtless) what so profoundly affected Keats
when he "heard Chapman speak out loud and bold." Whatever it was, it gave us what Coleridge pronounced the best
sonnet in our language; and Lang's admiration of Homer
has given us at least the next best. Of course there must be
something in poems that produce poems — in a poet whom
most poets confess their king. I hold (with Poe) that there
is no such thing as a *long* poem — a poem of the length of an
Epic. It must consist of poetic passages connected by *recitativo*, to use an opera word; but it is perhaps better for that.
If the writer cannot write "sustained" poetry the reader
probably could not read it. Anyhow, I vote for Homer.

I am passing well, but shall soon seek the mountains,
though I hope to be here when Scheff points his prow this
way. Would that you were sailing with him!

I've been hearing all about all of you, for Eva Crawford
has been among you "takin' notes," and Eva's piquant
comments on what and whom she sees are delicious reading. I should suppose that *you* would appreciate Eva —
most persons don't. She is the best letter writer of her sex —
who are all good letter writers — and she is much beside. I
may venture to whisper that you'd find her estimate of
your work and personality "not altogether displeasing."

Now that I'm about such matters, I shall enclose a note
to my friend Dr. Robertson, who runs an insanery at Liver-
more and is an interesting fellow with a ditto family and a
library that will make you pea-green with envy. Go out
and see him some day and take Scheff, or any friend, along —
he wants to know you. You won't mind the facts that he
thinks all poetry the secretion of a diseased brain, and that

the only reason he doesn't think all brains (except his own) diseased is the circumstance that not all secrete poetry.

* * *

Seriously, he is a good fellow and full of various knowledges that most of us wot not of.

> Sincerely yours,
>
> AMBROSE BIERCE.

ᔆ᯷ ᔆ᯷ ᔆ᯷

MY DEAR GEORGE,

I have a letter from * * *, who is in St. Louis, to which his progress has been more leisurely than I liked, considering that I am remaining away from my mountains only to meet him. However, he intimates an intention to come in a week. I wish you were with him.

Washington, D. C.,
June 14,
1904.

I am sending the W. of W. to Scribner's, as you suggest, and if it is not taken shall try the other mags in the order of your preference. But it's funny that you — *you* — should prefer the "popular" magazines and wish the work "illustrated." Be assured the illustrations will shock you if you get them.

* * *

I understand what you say about being bored by the persons whom your work in letters brings about your feet. The most *contented* years of my life lately were the two or three that I passed here before Washington folk found out that I was an author. The fact has leaked out, and although not a soul of them buys and reads my books some of them bore me insupportably with their ignorant compliments and unwelcome attentions. I fancy I'll have to "move on."

Tell Maid Marian to use gloves when modeling, or the clay will enter into her soul through her fingers and she become herself a Shape of Clay. My notion is that she

should work in a paste made of ashes-of-roses moistened
with nectar.

* * *

Sincerely yours,

AMBROSE BIERCE.

P. S. Does it bore you that I like you to know my friends?
Professor * * *'s widow (and daughter) are very dear to
me. She knows about you, and I've written her that I'd ask
you to call on her. You'll like them all right, but I have
another purpose. I want to know how they prosper; and
they are a little reticent about that. Maybe you could as-
certain indirectly by seeing how they live. I asked Grizzly
to do this but of course he didn't, the shaggy brute that
he is.   A. B.

⁓ ⁓ ⁓

DEAR GEORGE,

Haines' Falls,
Greene Co., N. Y.,
August 4,
1904.

I haven't written a letter, except on business, since leaving Washington, June 30 — no, not since Scheff's arrival
there. I now return to earth, and my first call is on you.

You'll be glad to know that I'm having a good time here
in the Catskills. I shall not go back so long as I can find an
open hotel.

* * *

I should like to hear from you about our — or rather
your — set in California, and especially about *you.* Do you
still dally with the Muse? Enclosed you will find two damning evidences of additional incapacity. *Harper's* now have
"A Wine of Wizardry," and they too will indubitably turn
it down. I shall then try *The Atlantic,* where it should have
gone in the first place; and I almost expect its acceptance.

I'm not working much — just loafing on my cottage
porch; mixing an occasional cocktail; infesting the forests,

knife in hand, in pursuit of the yellow-birch sapling that furnishes forth the walking stick like yours; and so forth. I knocked off work altogether for a month when Scheff came, and should like to do so for *you*. Are you never going to visit the scenes of your youth?

* * *

It is awfully sad — that latest visit of Death to the heart and home of poor Katie Peterson. Will you kindly assure her of my sympathy?

Love to all the Piedmontese. Sincerely yours,

AMBROSE BIERCE.

◦◦◦◦◦◦

MY DEAR GEORGE,

First, thank you for the knife and the distinction of membership in the Ancient and Honorable Order of Knifers. I have made little use of the blades and other appliances, but the corkscrew is in constant use.

Haines' Falls, Greene Co., N. Y., August 27, 1904.

I'm enclosing a little missive from the editor of *Harper's*. Please reserve these things awhile and sometime I may ask them of you to "point a moral or adorn a tale" about that poem. If we can't get it published I'd like to write for some friendly periodical a review of an unpublished poem, with copious extracts and a brief history of it. I think that would be unique.

I find the pictures of Marian interesting, but have the self-denial to keep only one of them—the prettiest one of course. Your own is rather solemn, but it will do for the title page of the Testimony, which is still my favorite reading.

Scheff showed me your verses on Katie's baby, and Katie has since sent them. They are very tender and beautiful. I would not willingly spare any of your "personal" poems — least of all, naturally, the one personal to me. Your success with them is exceptional. Yet the habit of writing them is perilous, as the many failures of great poets attest — Milton, for example, in his lines to Syriack Skinner, his lines to a baby that died a-bornin' and so forth. The reason is obvious, and you have yourself, with sure finger, pointed it out:

> "Remiss the ministry they bear
> Who serve her with divided heart;
> She stands reluctant to impart
> Her strength to purpose, end, or care."

When one is intent upon pleasing some mortal, one is less intent upon pleasing the immortal Muse. All this is said only by way of admonition for the future, not in criticism of the past. I'm a sinner myself in that way, but then I'm not a saint in any way, so my example doesn't count.

I don't mind * * * calling me a "dignified old gentleman"— indeed, that is what I have long aspired to be, but have succeeded only in the presence of strangers, and not always then. * * *

(I forgot to say that your poem is now in the hands of the editor of the Atlantic.)

Your determination to "boom" me almost frightens me. Great Scott! you've no notion of the magnitude of the task you undertake; the labors of Hercules were as nothing to it. Seriously, don't make any enemies that way; it is not worth while. And you don't know how comfortable I am in my obscurity. It is like being in "the shadow of a great rock in a weary land."

How goes the no sale of Shapes of Clay? I am slowly saving up a bit of money to recoup your friendly outlay. That's a new thing for me to do — the saving, I mean — and I rather enjoy the sensation. If it results in making a miser of me you will have to answer for it to many a worthy complainant.

Get thee behind me, Satan! — it is not possible for me to go to California yet. For one thing, my health is better here in the East; I have utterly escaped asthma this summer, and summer is my only "sickly season" here. In California I had the thing at any time o' year — even at Wright's. But it is my hope to end my days out there.

I don't think Millard was too hard on Kipling; it was no "unconscious" plagiarism; just a "straight steal."

About Prentice Mulford. I knew him but slightly and used to make mild fun of him as "Dismal Jimmy." That expressed my notion of his character and work, which was mostly prose platitudes. I saw him last in London, a member of the Joaquin Miller-Charles Warren Stoddard-Olive Harper outfit at 11 Museum Street, Bloomsbury Square. He married there a fool girl named Josie — forget her other name — with whom I think he lived awhile in hell, then freed himself, and some years afterward returned to this country and was found dead one morning in a boat at Sag Harbor. Peace to the soul of him. No, he was not a faker, but a conscientious fellow who mistook his vocation.

My friends have returned to Washington, but I expect to remain here a few weeks yet, infesting the woods, devastating the mountain larders, supervising the sunsets and guiding the stars in their courses. Then to New York, and finally to Washington. Please get busy with that fame o' yours so as to have the wealth to come and help me loaf.

I hope you don't mind the typewriter — *I* don't.

Convey my love to all the sweet ladies of your entourage and make my compliments also to the Gang. Sincerely yours,

AMBROSE BIERCE.

Washington,
October 5,
1904.

DEAR GEORGE,

Your latest was dated Sept. 10. I got it while alone in the mountains, but since then I have been in New York City and at West Point and — here. New York is too strenuous for me; it gets on my nerves.

* * *

Please don't persuade me to come to California — I mean don't *try* to, for I can't, and it hurts a little to say nay. There's a big bit of my heart there, but — O never mind the reasons; some of them would not look well on paper. One of them I don't mind telling; I would not live in a state under union labor rule. There is still one place where the honest American laboring man is not permitted to cut throats and strip bodies of women at his own sweet will. That is the District of Columbia.

I am anxious to read Lilith; please complete it.

I have another note of rejection for you. It is from * * *. Knowing that you will not bank on what he says about the Metropolitan, I enclose it. I've acted on his advising and sent the poem. It is about time for it to come back. Then I shall try the other magazines until the list is exhausted.

Did I return your Jinks verses? I know I read them and meant to send them back, but my correspondence and my papers are in such hopeless disorder that I'm all at sea on these matters. For aught I know I may have elaborately "answered" the letter that I think myself to be answering now. I liked the verses very temperately, not madly.

Of course you are right about the magazine editors not knowing poetry when they see it. But who does? I have not known more than a half-dozen persons in America that did, and none of them edited a magazine.

* * *

No, I did not write the "Urus-Agricola-Acetes stuff," though it was written *for* me and, I believe, at my suggestion. The author was "Jimmy" Bowman, of whose death I wrote a sonnet which is in Black Beetles. He and I used to have a lot of fun devising literary mischiefs, fighting sham battles with each other and so forth. He was a clever chap and a good judge of whiskey.

Yes, in The Cynic's Dictionary I did "jump from A to M." I had previously done the stuff in various papers as far as M, then lost the beginning. So in resuming I re-did that part (quite differently, of course) in order to have the thing complete if I should want to make a book of it. I guess the Examiner isn't running much of it, nor much of anything of mine.

* * *

I like your love of Keats and the early Coleridge.

Sincerely yours,

Ambrose Bierce.

My dear Davis,

The "bad eminence" of turning down Sterling's great poem is one that you will have to share with some of your esteemed fellow magazinists — for examples, the editors of the Atlantic, Harper's, Scribner's, The Century, and now the Metropolitan, all of the élite. All of these gentlemen, I believe, profess, as you do not, to know literature when they see it, and to deal in it.

The N. Y. American Office, Washington, D. C., October 12, 1904.

Well I profess to deal in it in a small way, and if Sterling will let me I propose some day to ask judgment between them and me.

Even *you* ask for literature — if my stories are literature, as you are good enough to imply. (By the way, all the leading publishers of the country turned down that book until they saw it published without them by a merchant in San Francisco and another sort of publishers in London, Leipzig and Paris.) Well, you wouldn't do a thing to one of my stories!

No, thank you; if I have to write rot, I prefer to do it for the newspapers, which make no false pretences and are frankly rotten, and in which the badness of a bad thing escapes detection or is forgotten as soon as it is cold.

I know how to write a story (of the "happy ending" sort) for magazine readers for whom literature is too good, but I will not do so so long as stealing is more honorable and interesting.

I've offered you the best stuff to be had — Sterling's poem — and the best that I am able to make; and now you must excuse me. I do not doubt that you really think that you would take "the kind of fiction that made 'Soldiers and Civilians' the most readable book of its kind in this country," and it is nice of you to put it that way; but neither do I doubt that you would find the story sent a different kind of fiction and, like the satire which you return to me, "out of the question." An editor who has a preformed opinion of the kind of stuff that he is going to get will always be disappointed with the stuff that he does get.

I know this from my early experience as an editor — before I learned that what I needed was, not any particular kind of stuff, but just the stuff of a particular kind of writer.

All this without any feeling, and only by way of explaining why I must ask you to excuse me.

Sincerely yours,

AMBROSE BIERCE.

DEAR GEORGE,
                            * * *

Yes, I got and read that fool thing in the August Critic. Washington, D. C.,
I found in it nothing worse than stupidity — no malice. December 6,
Doubtless you have not sounded the deeper deeps of stu- 1904.
pidity in critics, and so are driven to other motives to
explain their unearthly errors. I know from my own experience of long ago how hard it is to accept abominable
criticism, obviously (to the criticee) unfair, without attrib-
uting a personal mean motive; but the attribution is nearly
always erroneous, even in the case of a writer with so many
personal enemies as I. You will do well to avoid that weakness of the tyro. * * * has the infirmity in an apparently
chronic form. Poets, by reason of the sensibilities that
make them poets, are peculiarly liable to it. I can't see any
evidence that the poor devil of the Critic knew better.

The Wine of Wizardry is at present at the Booklovers'.
It should have come back ere this, but don't you draw any
happy augury from that: I'm sure they'll turn it down, and
am damning them in advance.

I had a postal from * * * a few days ago. He was in Paris.
I've written him only once, explaining by drawing his attention to the fact that one's reluctance to write a letter
increases in the ratio of the square of the distance it has to
go. I don't know why that is so, but it is — at least in my
case.
                            * * *

Yes, I'm in perfect health, barring a bit of insomnia at
times, and enjoy life as much as I ever did — except when
in love and the love prospering; that is to say, when it was
new.   Sincerely yours,

                            AMBROSE BIERCE.

Washington, D. C.,
December 8,
1904.
DEAR GEORGE,

This is the worst yet! This jobbernowl seems to think "The Wine of Wizardry" a story. It should "arrive" and be "dramatic" — the denouement being, I suppose, a particularly exciting example of the "happy ending."

My dear fellow, I'm positively ashamed to throw your pearls before any more of these swine, and I humbly ask your pardon for having done it at all. I guess the "Wine" will have to await the publication of your next book.

But I'd like to keep this fellow's note if you will kindly let me have it. Sometime, when the poem is published, I shall paste it into a little scrap book, with all the notes of rejection, and then if I know a man or two capable of appreciating the humor of the thing I can make merry over it with them.   Sincerely yours,

AMBROSE BIERCE.

❧ ❧ ❧

The Army and
Navy Club,
Washington, D. C.,
My permanent
address,
February 18,
1905.
DEAR GEORGE,

It's a long time since the date of your latest letter, but I've been doing two men's work for many weeks and have actually not found the leisure to write to my friends. As it is the first time that I've worked really hard for several years I ought not to complain, and don't. But I hope it will end with this session of Congress.

I think I did not thank you for the additional copies of your new book — the new edition. I wish it contained the new poem, "A Wine of Wizardry." I've given up trying to get it into anything. I related my failure to Mackay, of "Success," and he asked to be permitted to see it. "No," I replied, "you too would probably turn it down, and I will take no chances of losing the respect that I have for you." And I'd not show it to him. He declared his intention of getting it, though — which was just what I wanted him to do. But I dare say he didn't.

Yes, you sent me "The Sea Wolf." My opinion of it? Certainly — or a part of it. It is a most disagreeable book, as a whole. London has a pretty bad style and no sense of proportion. The story is a perfect welter of disagreeable incidents. Two or three (of the kind) would have sufficed to *show* the character of the man Larsen; and his own self-revealings by word of mouth would have "done the rest." Many of these incidents, too, are impossible — such as that of a man mounting a ladder with a dozen other men — more or less — hanging to his leg, and the hero's work of rerigging a wreck and getting it off a beach where it had stuck for weeks, and so forth. The "love" element, with its absurd suppressions and impossible proprieties, is awful. I confess to an overwhelming contempt for both the sexless lovers.

Now as to the merits. It is a rattling good story in one way; something is "going on" all the time — not always what one would wish, but *something*. One does not go to sleep over the book. But the great thing — and it is among the greatest of things — is that tremendous creation, Wolf Larsen. If that is not a permanent addition to literature, it is at least a permanent figure in the memory of the reader. You "can't lose" Wolf Larsen. He will be with you to the end. So it does not really matter how London has hammered him into you. You may quarrel with the methods, but the result is almost incomparable. The hewing out and setting up of such a figure is enough for a man to do in one life-time. I have hardly words to impart my good judgment of *that* work.

* * *

That is a pretty picture of Phyllis as Cleopatra — whom I

think you used to call "the angel child" — as the Furies were called Eumenides.

* * *

I'm enclosing a review of your book in the St. Louis "Mirror," a paper always kindly disposed toward our little group of gifted obscurians. I thought you might not have seen it; and it is worth seeing. Percival Pollard sends it me; and to him we owe our recognition by the "Mirror."

I hope you prosper apace. I mean mentally and spiritually; all other prosperity is trash.

Sincerely yours,

AMBROSE BIERCE.

Washington, D. C., April 17, 1905.

DEAR GEORGE,

I've reached your letter on my file. I wonder that I did, for truly I'm doing a lot of work — mostly of the pot-boiler, newspaper sort, some compiling of future — probably *very* future — books and a little for posterity.

Valentine has not returned the "Wine of Wizardry," but I shall tell him to in a few days and will then try it on the magazines you mention. If that fails I can see no objection to offering it to the English periodicals.

I don't know about Mackay. He has a trifle of mine which he was going to run months ago. He didn't and I asked it back. He returned it and begged that it go back to him for immediate publication. It went back, but publication did not ensue. In many other ways he has been exceedingly kind. Guess he can't always have his way.

* * *

I read that other book to the bitter end — the "Arthur Sterling" thing. He is the most disagreeable character in fiction, though Marie Bashkirtseff and Mary McLean in

real life could give him cards and spades. Fancy a poet, or
any kind of writer, whom it hurts to think! What the devil
are his agonies all about — his writhings and twistings and
foaming at all his mouths? What would a poem by an intellectual epileptic like that be? Happily the author spares
us quotation. I suppose there are Arthur Sterlings among
the little fellows, but if genius is not serenity, fortitude and
reasonableness I don't know what it is. One cannot even
imagine Shakespeare or Goethe bleeding over his work and
howling when "in the fell clutch of circumstance." The
great ones are figured in my mind as ever smiling — a little
sadly at times, perhaps, but always with conscious inaccessibility to the pinpricking little Titans that would storm
their Olympus armed with ineffectual disasters and pop-
gun misfortunes. Fancy a fellow wanting, like Arthur Sterling, to be supported by his fellows in order that he may
write what they don't want to read! Even Jack London
would gag at such Socialism as *that*.

* * *

I'm going to pass a summer month or two with the Pol-
lards, at Saybrook, Conn. How I wish you could be of the
party. But I suppose you'll be chicken-ranching then, and
happy enough where you are. I wish you joy of the venture
and, although I fear it means a meagre living, it will probably be more satisfactory than doubling over a desk in your
uncle's office. The very name Carmel Bay is enchanting.
I've a notion I shall see that ranch some day. I don't quite
recognize the "filtered-through-the-emasculated-minds-of-
about-six-fools" article from which you say I quote — don't
remember it, nor remember quoting from it.

I don't wonder at your surprise at my high estimate of
Longfellow in a certain article. It is higher than my perma-

nent one. I was thinking (while writing for a newspaper, recollect) rather of his fame than of his genius — I had to have a literary equivalent to Washington or Lincoln. Still, we must not forget that Longfellow wrote "Chrysaor" and, in narrative poetry (which you don't care for) "Robert of Sicily." Must one be judged by his average, or may he be judged, on occasion, by his highest? He is strongest who can lift the greatest weight, not he who habitually lifts lesser ones.

As to your queries. So far as I know, Realf *did* write his great sonnets on the night of his death. Anyhow, they were found with the body. Your recollection that I said they were written before he came to the Coast is faulty. Some of his other things were in print when he submitted them to me (and took pay for them) as new; but not the "De Mortuis."

I got the lines about the echoes (I *think* they go this way:

"the loon
Laughed, and the echoes, huddling in affright,
Like Odin's hounds went baying down the night")

fiom a poem entitled, I think, "The Washers of the Shroud." I found it in the "Atlantic," in the summer of 1864, while at home from the war suffering from a wound, and — disgraceful fact! — have never seen nor heard of it since. If the magazine was a current number, as I suppose, it should be easy to find the poem. If you look it up tell me about it. I don't even know the author — had once a vague impression that it was Lowell but don't know.

The compound "mulolatry," which I made in "Ashes of the Beacon," would not, of course, be allowable in composition altogether serious. I used it because I could not at the moment think of the right word, "gyneolatry," or

"gynecolatry," according as you make use of the nomina-
tive or the accusative. I once made "caniolatry" for a
similar reason — just laziness. It's not nice to do things o'
that kind, even in newspapers.

* * *

I had intended to write you something of "beesness," but
time is up and it must wait. This letter is insupportably
long already.

My love to Carrie and Katie. Sincerely yours,

AMBROSE BIERCE.

๑ ๑ ๑

DEAR GEORGE,

Bailey Millard is editor of "The Cosmopolitan Magazine," which Mr. Hearst has bought. I met him in New
York two weeks ago. He had just arrived and learning from
Hearst that I was in town looked me up. I had just recom-
mended him to Hearst as editor. He had intended him for
associate editor. I think that will give you a chance, such as
it is. Millard dined with me and I told him the adventures
of "A Wine of Wizardry." I shall send it to him as soon as
he has warmed his seat, unless you would prefer to send it
yourself. He already knows my whole good opinion of it,
and he shares my good opinion of you.

Army and Navy Club,
Washington, D. C.,
May 16,
1905.

I suppose you are at your new ranch, but I shall address
this letter as usual.

* * *

If you hear of my drowning know that it is the natural
(and desirable) result of the canoe habit. I've a dandy
canoe and am tempting fate and alarming my friends by
frequenting, not the margin of the upper river, but the
broad reaches below town, where the wind has miles and
miles of sweep and kicks up a most exhilarating combob-

bery. If I escape I'm going to send my boat up to Say-brook, Connecticut, and navigate Long Island Sound.

Are you near enough to the sea to do a bit of boating now and then? When I visit you I shall want to bring my canoe.

I've nearly given up my newspaper work, but shall do something each month for the Magazine. Have not done much yet — have not been in the mind. Death has been striking pretty close to me again, and you know how that upsets a fellow.   Sincerely yours,

AMBROSE BIERCE.

Washington,
June 16,
1905.

DEAR GEORGE,

I'm your debtor for two good long letters. You err in thinking your letters, of whatever length and frequency, can be otherwise than delightful to me.

No, you had not before sent me Upton Sinclair's article explaining why American literature is "bourgeois." It is amusingly grotesque. The political and economical situation has about as much to do with it as have the direction of our rivers and the prevailing color of our hair. But it is of the nature of the faddist (and of all faddists the ultra socialist is the most untamed by sense) to see in everything his hobby, with its name writ large. He is the humorist of observers. When Sinclair transiently forgets his gospel of the impossible he can see well enough.

I note what you say of * * * and know that he did not use to like me, though I doubt if he ever had any antipathy to you. Six or eight years ago I tackled him on a particularly mean fling that he had made at me while I was absent from California. (I think I had not met him before.) I told him, rather coarsely, what I thought of the matter. He candidly confessed himself in the wrong, expressed regret and has ever since, so far as I know, been just and even generous to me. I think him sincere now, and enclose a letter which seems to show it. You may return it if you will — I send it mainly because it concerns your poem. The trouble — our trouble — with * * * is that he has voluntarily entered into slavery to the traditions and theories of the magazine trade, which, like those of all trades, are the product of small men. The big man makes his success by ignoring them. Your estimate of * * * I'm not disposed to quarrel with, but do think him pretty square.

* * *

Bless you, don't take the trouble to go through the Iliad and Odyssey to pick out the poetical parts. I grant you they are brief and infrequent — I mean in the translation. I hold, with Poe, that there are no long poems — only bursts of poetry in long spinnings of metrical prose. But even the "recitativo" of the translated Grecian poets has a charm to one that it may not have to another. I doubt if any-one who has always loved "the glory that was Greece" — who has been always in love with its jocund deities, and so forth, can say accurately just how much of his joy in Homer (for example) is due to love of poetry, and how much to a renewal of mental youth and young illusions. Some part of the delight that we get from verse defies analysis and classification. Only a man without a memory (and memories) could say just what pleased him in poetry and be sure that it was the poetry only. For example, I never read the opening lines of the Pope Iliad — and I don't need the book for much of the first few hundred, I guess — without seeming to be on a sunny green hill on a cold windy day, with the bluest of skies above me and billows of pasture below, running to a clean-cut horizon. There's nothing in the text warranting that illusion, which is nevertheless to me a *part* of the Iliad; a most charming part, too. It all comes of my having first read the thing under such conditions at the age of about ten. I *remember* that; but how many times I must be powerfully affected by the poets *without* remembering why. If a fellow could cut out all that extrinsic interest he would be a fool to do so. But he would be a better critic.

You ought to be happy in the contemplation of a natural, wholesome life at Carmel Bay — the "prospect pleases," surely. But I fear, I fear. Maybe you can get a newspaper connection that will bring you in a small income without compelling you to do violence to your literary conscience. I doubt if you can get your living out of the ground. But I shall watch the experiment with sympathetic interest, for it "appeals" to me. I'm a trifle jaded with age and the urban life, and maybe if you can succeed in that other sort of thing I could.

* * *

As to * * * the Superb. Isn't Sag Harbor somewhere near Saybrook, Connecticut, at the mouth of the river of that name? I'm going there for a month with Percival Pollard. Shall leave here about the first of July. If Sag Harbor is easily accessible from there, and * * * would care to see me, I'll go and call on her. * * * But maybe I'd fall in love with her and, being now (alas) eligible, just marry her alive! — or be turned down by her, to the unspeakable wrecking of my peace! I'm only a youth — 63 on the 24th of this month — and it would be too bad if I got started wrong in life. But really I don't know about the good taste of being jocular about * * *. I'm sure she must be a serious enough maiden, with the sun of a declining race yellow on her hair. Eva Crawford thinks her most lovable — and Eva has a clear, considering eye upon you all.

* * *

I'm going to send up my canoe to Saybrook and challenge the rollers of the Sound. Don't you fear — I'm an expert canoeist from boyhood. * * *   Sincerely,

AMBROSE BIERCE.

ᕼᕼ ᕼᕼ ᕼᕼ

DEAR GEORGE,

I have at last the letter that I was waiting for — didn't answer the other, for one of mine was on the way to you.

Washington, D. C., December 3, 1905.

* * *

You need not worry yourself about your part of the business. You have acted "mighty white," as was to have been expected of you; and, caring little for any other feature of the matter, I'm grateful to you for giving my pessimism and growing disbelief in human disinterestedness a sound wholesome thwack on the mazzard.

* * *

Yes, I was sorry to whack London, for whom, in his character as author, I have a high admiration, and in that of publicist and reformer a deep contempt. Even if he had been a personal friend, I should have whacked him, and doubtless much harder. I'm not one of those who give their friends carte blanche to sin. If my friend dishonors himself he dishonors me; if he makes a fool of himself he makes a fool of me — which another cannot do.

* * *

Your description of your new environment, in your other letter, makes me "homesick" to see it. I cordially congratulate you and Mrs. Sterling on having the sense to do what I have always been too indolent to do — namely as you please. Guess I've been always too busy "warming both hands before the fire of life." And now, when

"It sinks and I am ready to depart,"

I find that the damned fire was in *me* and ought to have been quenched with a dash of cold sense. I'm having my canoe decked and yawl-rigged for deep water and live in the hope of being drowned according to the dictates of my conscience.

By way of proving my power of self-restraint I'm going to stop this screed with a whole page unused.

Sincerely yours, as ever,
Ambrose Bierce.

ॐ ॐ ॐ

Washington, D. C.,
February 3,
1906. Dear George,

I don't know why I've not written to you — that is, I don't know why God made me what I have the misfortune to be: a sufferer from procrastination.

* * *

I have read Mary Austin's book with unexpected interest. It is pleasing exceedingly. You may not know that I'm familiar with the *kind* of country she writes of, and reading the book was like traversing it again. But the best of her is her style. That is delicious. It has a slight "tang" of archaism — just enough to suggest "lucent sirups tinct with cinnamon," or the "spice and balm" of Miller's sea-winds. And what a knack at observation she has! Nothing escapes her eye. Tell me about her. What else has she written? What is she going to write? If she is still young she will do great work; if not — well, she *has* done it in that book. But she'll have to hammer and hammer again and again before the world will hear and heed.

As to me I'm pot-boiling. My stuff in the N. Y. American (I presume that the part of it that you see is in the Examiner) is mere piffle, written without effort, purpose or care. My department in the Cosmopolitan is a failure, as I told Millard it would be. It is impossible to write topical stuff for a magazine. How can one discuss with heart or inspiration a thing that happens two months or so before one's comments on it will be read? The venture and the title were Hearst's notion, but the title so handicaps me that I can do nothing right. I shall drop it.

I've done three little stories for the March number (they may be postponed) that are ghastly enough to make a pig squeal.   * * *

Sincerely yours,

AMBROSE BIERCE.

MY DEAR GEORGE,

First, about the "Wine," I dislike the "privately printed" racket. Can you let the matter wait a little longer? Neale has the poem, and Neale is just now inaccessible to letters, somewhere in the South in the interest of his magazine-that-is-to-be. I called when in New York, but he had flown and I've been unable to reach him; but he is due here on the 23rd. Then if his mag is going to hold fire, or if he doesn't want the poem for it, let Robertson or Josephare have a hack at it.

Washington, D. C., March 12, 1906.

Barr is amusing. I don't care to have a copy of his remarks.

About the pirating of my stories. That is a matter for Chatto and Windus, who bought the English copyright of the book from which that one story came. I dare say, though, the publication was done by arrangement with them. Anyhow my interests are not involved.

I was greatly interested in your account of Mrs. Austin. She's a clever woman and should write a good novel—if there is such a thing as a good novel. I won't read novels.

Yes, the "Cosmopolitan" cat-story is Leigh's and is to be credited to him if ever published in covers. I fathered it as the only way to get it published at all. Of course I had to rewrite it; it was very crude and too horrible. A story may be terrible, but must not be horrible—there is a difference. I found the manuscript among his papers.

It is disagreeable to think of the estrangement between * * * and his family. Doubtless the trouble arises from his being married. Yes, it is funny, his taking his toddy along with you old soakers. I remember he used to kick at my having wine in camp and at your having a bottle hidden away in the bushes.

I had seen that group of you and Joaquin and Stoddard and laughed at your lifelike impersonation of the Drowsy Demon.

I passed the first half of last month in New York. Went there for a dinner and stayed to twelve. Sam Davis and Homer Davenport were of the party.

Sam was here for a few days—but maybe you don't know Sam. He's a brother to Bob, who swears you got your Dante-like solemnity of countenance by coming into his office when he was editing a newspaper.

You are not to think I have thrown * * * over. There are only two or three matters of seriousness between us and they cannot profitably be discussed in letters, so they must wait until he and I meet if we ever do. I shall mention them to no one else and I don't suppose he will to anyone but me. Apart from these—well, our correspondence was disagreeable, so the obvious thing to do was to put an end to it. To unlike a friend is not an easy thing to do, and I've not attempted to do it.

Of course I approve the new lines in the "Wine" and if Neale or anybody else will have the poem I shall insert them in their place. That "screaming thing" stays with one almost as does "the blue-eyed vampire," and is not only visible, as is she, but audible as well. If you go on adding lines to the poem I shall not so sharply deplore our failure to get it into print. As Mark Twain says: "Every time you draw you fill."

The "Night in Heaven" is fine work in the grand style and its swing is haunting when one gets it. I get a jolt or two in the reading, but I dare say you purposely contrived them and I can't say they hurt. Of course the rhythm recalls Kipling's "The Last Chanty" (I'm not sure I spell the word correctly—if there's a correct way) but that is nothing. Nobody has the copyright of any possible metre or rhythm in English prosody. It has been long since anybody was "first." When are you coming to Washington to sail in my canoe? Sincerely yours,   AMBROSE BIERCE.

ᴐ⊙⊷ ᴐ⊙⊷ ᴐ⊙⊷

DEAR GEORGE,

I've been in New York again but am slowly recovering. I saw Neale. He assures me that the magazine will surely materialize about June, and he wants the poem, "A Wine of Wizardry," with an introduction by me. I think he means it; if so that will give it greater publicity than what you have in mind, even if the mag eventually fail. Magazines if well advertised usually sell several hundred thousand of the first issue; the trick is to keep them going. Munsey's "Scrap Book" disposed of a half-million. * * *

* * * was to start for a few weeks in California about

Washington, D. C., April 5, 1906.

now. I hope you will see him. He is not a bad lot when convinced that one respects him. He has been treated pretty
badly in this neck o' the woods, as is every Western man
who breaks into this realm of smugwumps.

My benediction upon Carmelites all and singular — if any
are all.   Sincerely yours,

AMBROSE BIERCE.

Doubleday, Page & Co. are to publish my "Cynic's Dictionary."

꙼꙼꙼

DEAR GEORGE,

I write in the hope that you are alive and the fear that
you are wrecked.*

Please let me know if I can help — I need not say how
glad I shall be to do so. "Help" would go with this were I
sure about you and the post-office. It's a mighty bad business and one does not need to own property out there to be
"hit hard" by it. One needs only to have friends there.

We are helpless here, so far as the telegraph is concerned —
shall not be able to get anything on the wires for many
days, all private dispatches being refused.

Pray God you and yours may be all right. Of course anything that you may be able to tell me of my friends will be
gratefully received. Sincerely yours, AMBROSE BIERCE.

꙼꙼꙼

DEAR GEORGE,

Your letter relieves me greatly. I had begun to fear that
you had "gone before." Thank you very much for your
news of our friends. I had already heard from Eva Croffie.
Also from Grizzly.   * * *

Thank you for Mr. Eddy's review of "Shapes." But he is

*The San Francisco earthquake and fire had occurred April 18, 1906.

misinformed about poor Flora Shearer. Of course I helped her — who would not help a good friend in adversity? But she went to Scotland to a brother long ago, and at this time I do not know if she is living or dead.

But here am I forgetting (momentarily) that awful wiping out of San Francisco. It "hit" me pretty hard in many ways — mostly indirectly, through my friends. I had rather hoped to have to "put up" for you and your gang, and am a trifle disappointed to know that you are all right — except the chimneys. I'm glad that tidal wave did not come, but don't you think you'd better have a canoe ready? You could keep it on your veranda stacked with provisions and whiskey.

My letter from Ursus (written during the conflagration) expresses a keen solicitude for the Farallones, as the fire was working westward.

If this letter is a little disconnected and incoherent know, O King, that I have just returned from a dinner in Atlantic City, N. J. I saw Markham there, also Bob Davis, Sam Moffett, Homer Davenport, Bob Mackay and other San Franciscans. (Can there be a San Franciscan when there is no San Francisco? I don't want to go back. Doubtless the new San Francisco — while it lasts — will be a finer town than the old, but it will not be *my* San Francisco and I don't want to see it. It has for many years been, to me, full of ghosts. Now it is itself a ghost.)

I return the sonnets. Destruction of "Town Talk" has doubtless saved you from having the one on me turned down. Dear old fellow, don't take the trouble to defend my memory when — or at least until —

> "I am fled
> From this vile world, with vilest worms to dwell."

I'm not letting my enemies' attitude trouble me at all. On the contrary, I'm rather sorry for them and their insomnia — lying awake o' nights to think out new and needful lies about me, while I sleep sweetly. O, it is all right, truly.

No, I never had any row (nor much acquaintance) with Mark Twain — met him but two or three times. Once with Stoddard in London. I think pretty well of him, but doubt if he cared for me and can't, at the moment, think of any reason why he *should* have cared for me.

"The Cynic's Dictionary" is a-printing. I shall have to call it something else, for the publishers tell me there is a "Cynic's Dictionary" already out. I dare say the author took more than my title — the stuff has been a rich mine for a plagiarist for many a year. They (the publishers) won't have "The Devil's Dictionary." Here in the East the Devil is a sacred personage (the Fourth Person of the Trinity, as an Irishman might say) and his name must not be taken in vain.

No, "The Testimony of the Suns" has not "palled" on me. I still read it and still think it one of the world's greatest poems.   * * *

Well, God be wi' ye and spare the shack at Carmel,
Sincerely yours,
* * *   AMBROSE BIERCE.

❦ ❦ ❦

Washington, D. C.,   DEAR GEORGE,
June 11,
1906.   Your poem, "A Dream of Fear" was so good before that it needed no improvement, though I'm glad to observe that you have "the passion for perfection." Sure — you shall have your word "colossal" applied to a thing of two dimensions, an you will.

I have no objection to the publication of that sonnet on me. It may give my enemies a transient feeling that is disagreeable, and if I can do that without taking any trouble in the matter myself it is worth doing. I think they must have renewed their activity, to have provoked you so — got up a new and fascinating lie, probably. Thank you for putting your good right leg into action themward.

What a "settlement" you have collected about you at Carmel! All manner of cranks and curios, to whom I feel myself drawn by affinity. Still I suppose I shall not go. I should have to see the new San Francisco — when it has foolishly been built — and I'd rather not. One does not care to look upon either the mutilated face of one's mashed friend or an upstart imposter bearing his name. No, *my* San Francisco is gone and I'll have no other.

* * *

You are wrong about Gorky — he has none of the "artist" in him. He is not only a peasant, but an anarchist and an advocate of assassination — by others; like most of his tribe, he doesn't care to take the risk himself. His "career" in this country has been that of a yellow dog. Hearst's newspapers and * * * are the only friends that remain to him of all those that acclaimed him when he landed. And all the sturdy lying of the former cannot rehabilitate him. It isn't merely the woman matter. You'd understand if you were on this side of the country. I was myself a dupe in the matter. He had expressed high admiration of my books (in an interview in Russia) and when his Government released him from prison I cabled him congratulations. O, my!

Yes, I've observed the obviously lying estimates of the San Franciscan dead; also that there was no earthquake — just a fire; also the determination to "beat" the insurance companies. Insurance is a hog game, and if they (the companies) can be beaten out of their dishonest gains by superior dishonesty I have no objection; but in my judgment they are neither legally nor morally liable for the half that is claimed of them. Those of them that took no earthquake risks don't owe a cent.

Please don't send * * *'s verses to me if you can decently decline. I should be sorry to find them bad, and my loathing of the Whitmaniacal "form" is as deep as yours. Perhaps I should find them good otherwise, but the probability is so small that I don't want to take the chance.

* * *

I've just finished reading the first proofs of "The Cynic's Word Book," which Doubleday, Page & Co. are to bring out in October. My dealings with them have been most pleasant and one of them whom I met the other day at Atlantic City seems a fine fellow.

I think I told you that S. O. Howes, of Galveston, Texas, is compiling a book of essays and sich from some of my stuff that I sent him. I've left the selection entirely to him and presented him with the profits if there be any. He'll probably not even find a publisher. He has the work about half done. By the way, he is an enthusiastic admirer of you. For that I like him, and for much else.

I mean to stay here all summer if I die for it, as I probably shall. Luck and love to you.

Sincerely yours,

Ambrose Bierce.

❧ ❧ ❧

The Army and Navy Club, Washington, D. C., June 20, 1906.

Dear Mr. Cahill,

I am more sorry than I can say to be unable to send you the copy of the Builder's Review that you kindly sent *me*.

But before receiving your note I had, in my own interest, searched high and low for it, in vain. Somebody stole it from my table. I especially valued it after the catastrophe, but should have been doubly pleased to have it for you.

It was indeed a rough deal you San Franciscans got. I had always expected to go back to the good old town some day, but I have no desire to see the new town, if there is to be one. I fear the fire consumed even the ghosts that used to meet me at every street corner — ghosts of dear dead friends, oh, so many of them!

Please accept my sympathy for your losses. I too am a "sufferer," a whole edition of my latest book, plates and all, having gone up in smoke and many of my friends being now in the "dependent class." It hit us all pretty hard, I guess, wherever we happened to be.

Sincerely yours,
AMBROSE BIERCE.

ᔑ᙮ ᔑ᙮ ᔑ᙮

DEAR GEORGE,
* * *

If your neighbor Carmelites are really "normal" and respectable I'm sorry for you. They will surely (remaining cold sober themselves) drive you to drink. Their sort affects *me* that way. God bless the crank and the curio! — what would life in this desert be without its mullahs and its dervishes? A matter of merchants and camel drivers — no one to laugh with and at.

Did you see Gorky's estimate of us in "Appleton's"? Having been a few weeks in the land, whose language he knows not a word of, he knows (by intuition of genius and a wee-bit help from Gaylord Wilshire and his gang) all about us, and tells it in generalities of vituperation as ap-

Washington, D. C.,
August 11,
1906.

plicable to one country as to another. He's a dandy bomb-thrower, but he handles the stink-pot only indifferently well. He should write (for "The Cosmopolitan") on "The Treason of God."

Sorry you didn't like my remarks in that fool "symposium." If I said enough to make it clear that I don't care a damn for any of the matters touched upon, nor for the fellows who *do* care, I satisfied my wish. It was not intended to be an "argument" at all — at least not on my part; I don't argue with babes and sucklings. Hunter is a decentish fellow, for a dreamer, but the Hillquit person is a humorless anarchist. When I complimented him on the beauty of his neck and expressed the hope of putting a nice, new rope about it he nearly strangled on the brandy that I was putting down it at the hotel bar. And it wasn't with merriment. His anarchist sentiments were all cut out.

I'm not familiar with the poetry of William Vaughan Moody. Can you "put me on"?

I'm sending you an odd thing by Eugene Wood, of Niagara Falls, where I met him two or three years ago. I'm sure you will appreciate it. The poor chap died the other day and might appropriately — as he doubtless will — lie in a neglected grave. You may return the book when you have read it enough. I'm confident you never heard of it.

Enclosed is your sonnet, with a few suggestions of no importance. I had not space on it to say that the superfluity of superlatives noted, is accentuated by the words "west" and "quest" immediately following, making a lot of "ests." The verses are pleasing, but if any villain prefer them to "In Extremis" may he bite himself with a Snake!

If you'll send me that shuddery thing on Fear — with the "clangor of ascending chains" line — and one or two others that you'd care to have in a magazine, I'll try them on Maxwell. I suspect he will fall dead in the reading, or possibly dislocate the jaw of him with a yawn, but even so you will not have written in vain.

Have you tried anything on "Munsey"? Bob Davis is the editor, and we talked you over at dinner (where would you could have been). I think he values my judgment a little.* * *

I wish I could be blown upon by your Carmel sea-breeze; the weather here is wicked! I don't even canoe.

My "Cynic" book is due in October. Shall send it to you.

Sincerely yours,

AMBROSE BIERCE.

୬◖ ୬◖ ୬◖

DEAR GEORGE,

Both your letters at hand.

* * *

Be a "magazine poet" all you can — that is the shortest road to recognition, and all our greater poets have travelled it. You need not compromise with your conscience, however, by writing "magazine poetry." You couldn't. *Washington, D. C., September 28, 1906.*

What's your objection to * * * ? I don't observe that it is greatly worse than others of its class. But a fellow who has for nigh upon twenty years written for yellow newspapers can't be expected to say much that's edifying on that subject. So I dare say I'm wrong in my advice about the *kind* of swine for your pearls. There are probably more than the two kinds of pigs — live ones and dead ones.

Yes, I'm a colonel — in Pennsylvania Avenue. In the neighborhood of my tenement I'm a Mister. At my club I'm a major — which is my real title by an act of Congress. I suppressed it in California, but couldn't here, where I run with the military gang.

You need not blackguard your poem, "A Visitor," though I could wish you had not chosen blank verse. That form seems to me suitable (in serious verse) only to lofty, not lowly, themes. Anyhow, I always expect something pretty high when I begin an unknown poem in blank. Moreover, it is not your best "medium." Your splendid poem, "Music," does not wholly commend itself to me for that reason. May I say that it is a little sing-songy—the lines monotonously alike in their caesural pauses and some of their other features?

By the way, I'd like to see what you could do in more unsimple meters than the ones that you handle so well. The wish came to me the other day in reading Lanier's "The Marshes of Glynn" and some of his other work. Lanier did not often equal his master, Swinburne, in getting the most out of the method, but he did well in the poem mentioned. Maybe you could manage the dangerous thing. It would be worth doing and is, therefore, worth trying.

Thank you for the Moody book, which I will return. He pleaseth me greatly and I could already fill pages with analyses of him for the reasons therefore. But for you to say that he has *you* "skinned" — that is magnanimity. An excellent thing in poets, I grant you, and a rare one. There is something about him and his book in the current "Atlantic," by May Sinclair, who, I dare say, has never heard of *you*. Unlike you, she thinks his dramatic work the best of what he does. I've not seen that. To be the best it must be mighty good.

Yes, poor White's poetry is all you say — and worse, but, faith! he "had it in him." What struck me was his candid apotheosis of piracy on the high seas. I'd hate the fellow who hadn't some sneaking sympathy with that—as Goethe confessed to some sympathy with every vice. Nobody'll ever hear of White, but (pray observe, ambitious bard!) he isn't caring. How wise are the dead!

* * *

My friend Howes, of Galveston, has, I think, nearly finished compiling his book of essaylets from my stuff. Neale has definitely decided to bring out "The Monk and the Hangman's Daughter." He has the plates of my two luckless Putnam books, and is figuring on my "complete works," to be published by subscription. I doubt if he will undertake it right away.

Au reste, I'm in good health and am growing old not altogether disgracefully.   Sincerely yours,

AMBROSE BIERCE.

๛ ๛ ๛

DEAR GEORGE,

I'm pained by your comments on my book. I always feel that way when praised — "just plunged in a gulf of dark despair" to think that I took no more trouble to make the commendation truer. I shall try harder with the Howes book.

The Army and Navy Club, Washington, October 30, 1906.

* * *

I can't supply the missing link between pages 101 and 102 of the "Word Book," having destroyed the copy and proofs. Supply it yourself.

You err: the book is getting me a little glory, but that will be all — it will have no sale, for it has no slang, no "dialect" and no grinning through a horse-collar. By the way, please send me any "notices" of it that you may chance to see out there.

* * *

I've done a ghost story for the January "Cosmopolitan,"

which I think pretty well of. That's all I've done for more than two months.

I return your poem and the Moody book. Sincerely yours,

AMBROSE BIERCE.

❧ ❧ ❧

The Army and
Navy Club,
Washington,
December 5,
1906.
DEAR GEORGE,

Your letter of Nov. 28 has just come to my breakfast table. It is the better part of the repast.

* * *

No, my dictionary will not sell. I so assured the publishers.

I lunched with Neale the other day — he comes down here once a month. His magazine (I think he is to call it "The Southerner," or something like that) will not get out this month, as he expected it to. And for an ominous reason: He had relied largely on Southern writers, and finds that they can't write! He assures me that it *will* appear this winter and asked me not to withdraw your poem and my remarks on it unless you asked it. So I did not.

* * *

In your character of bookseller carrying a stock of my books you have a new interest. May Heaven promote you to publisher!

Thank you for the Moody books — which I'll return soon. "The Masque of Judgment" has some great work in its final pages — quite as great as anything in Faust. The passages that you marked are good too, but some of them barely miss being entirely satisfying. It would trouble you to find many such passages in the other book, which is, moreover, not distinguished for clarity. I found myself frequently prompted to ask the author: "What the devil are you driving at?"

I'm going to finish this letter at home where there is less talk of the relative military strength of Japan and San Francisco and the latter power's newest and most grievous affliction, Teddy Roosevelt. AMBROSE BIERCE.

P. S. Guess the letter is finished.

◦◦◦ ◦◦◦ ◦◦◦

DEAR GEORGE,

I suppose I owe you letters and letters — but you don't particularly like to write letters yourself, so you'll understand.

The Army and Navy Club, Washington, D. C., January 27, 1907.

* * *

Hanging before me is a water-color of a bit of Carmel Beach, by Chris Jorgensen, for which I blew in fifty dollars the other day. He had a fine exhibition of his Californian work here. I wanted to buy it all, but compromised with my desire by buying what I could. The picture has a sentimental value to me, apart from its artistic.

* * *

I am to see Neale in a few days and shall try to learn definitely when his magazine is to come out — if he knows. If he does not I'll withdraw your poem. Next month he is to republish "The Monk and the Hangman's Daughter," with a new preface which somebody will not relish. I'll send you a copy. The Howes book is on its travels among the publishers, and so, doubtless, will long continue.

Sincerely yours,

AMBROSE BIERCE.

◦◦◦ ◦◦◦ ◦◦◦

DEAR GEORGE,

Our letters "crossed" — a thing that "happens" oftener than not in my correspondence, when neither person has written for a long time. I have drawn some interesting in-

The Army and Navy Club, Washington, D. C., February 5, 1907.

ferences from this fact, but have no time now to state them. Indeed, I have no time to do anything but send you the stuff on the battle of Shiloh concerning which you inquire.

I should write it a little differently now, but it may entertain you as it is.   * * *

Sincerely yours,

* * *   AMBROSE BIERCE.

ᕲ᷊ ᕲ᷊ ᕲ᷊

Washington,
February 21,
1907. MY DEAR GEORGE,

If you desert Carmel I shall destroy my Jorgensen picture, build a bungalow in the Catskills and cut out California forever. (Those are the footprints of my damned canary, who will neither write himself nor let me write. Just now he is perched on my shoulder, awaiting the command to sing — then he will deafen me with a song without sense. O he's a poet all right.)

I entirely approve your allegiance to Mammon. If I'd had brains enough to make a decision like that I could now, at 65, have the leisure to make a good book or two before I go to the waste-dump. * * * Get yourself a fat bank account — there's no such friend as a bank account, and the greatest book is a check-book; "You may lay to that!" as one of Stevenson's pirates puts it.

* * *

No, sir, your boss will not bring you East next June; or if he does you will not come to Washington. How do I know? I don't know how I know, but concerning all (and they are many) who were to come from California to see me I have never once failed in my forecast of their coming or not coming. Even in the case of * * *, although I wrote to you, and to her, as if I expected her, I *said* to one of my friends: "She will not come." I don't think it's a gift of divination — it just happens, somehow. Yours is not a very good example, for you have not said you were coming, "sure."

So your colony of high-brows is re-establishing itself at the old stand — Piedmont. * * * But Piedmont — it must be in the heart of Oakland. I could no longer shoot rabbits in the gulch back of it and sleep under a tree to shoot more in the morning. Nor could I traverse that long ridge with various girls. I dare say there's a boulevard running the length of it,

"A palace and a prison on each hand."

If I could stop you from reading that volume of old "Argonauts" I'd do so, but I suppose an injunction would not "lie." Yes, I was a slovenly writer in those days, though enough better than my neighbors to have attracted my own attention. My knowledge of English was imperfect "a whole lot." Indeed, my intellectual status (whatever it may be, and God knows it's enough to make me blush) was of slow growth — as was my moral. I mean, I had not literary sincerity.

Yes, I wrote of Swinburne the distasteful words that you quote. But they were not altogether untrue. He used to set my teeth on edge — could *not* stand still a minute, and kept you looking for the string that worked his legs and arms. And he had a weak face that gave you the memory of chinlessness. But I have long renounced the views that I once held about his poetry — held, or thought I held. I don't remember, though, if it was as lately as '78 that I held them.

You write of Miss Dawson. Did she survive the 'quake?

And do you know about her? Not a word of her has reached me. Notwithstanding your imported nightingale (upon which I think you should be made to pay a stiff duty) your Ina Coolbrith poem is so good that I want to keep it if you have another copy. I find no amendable faults in it. * * *

The fellow that told you that I was an editor of "The Cosmopolitan" has an impediment in his veracity. I simply write for it, * * *, and the less of my stuff the editor uses the better I'm pleased.   * * *

O, you ask about the "Ursus-Aborn-Gorgias-Agrestis-Polyglot" stuff. It was written by James F. ("Jimmie") Bowman — long dead. (See a pretty bad sonnet on page 94, "Shapes of Clay.") My only part in the matter was to suggest the papers and discuss them with him over many mugs of beer.   * * *

By the way, Neale says he gets almost enough inquiries for my books (from San Francisco) to justify him in republishing them.   * * *

That's all—and, as George Augustus Sala wrote of a chew of tobacco as the price of a certain lady's favors, "God knows it's enough!"   AMBROSE BIERCE.

⚬⚬ ⚬⚬ ⚬⚬

The Army and Navy Club, Washington, D. C., April 23, 1907.

DEAR GEORGE,

I have your letter of the 13th. The enclosed slip from the Pacific Monthly (thank you for it) is amusing. Yes, * * * is an insufferable pedant, but I don't at all mind his pedantry. Any critic is welcome to whack me all he likes if he will append to his remarks (as * * * had the thoughtfulness to do) my definition of "Critic" from the "Word Book."

Please don't bother to write me when the spirit does not move you thereto. You and I don't need to write to each other for any other reason than that we want to. As to coming East, abstain, O, abstain from promises, lest you resemble all my other friends out there, who promise always and never come. It would be delightful to see you here, but I know how those things arrange themselves without reference to our desires. We do as we must, not as we will.

I think that uncle of yours must be a mighty fine fellow. Be good to him and don't kick at his service, even when you feel the chain. It beats poetry for nothing a year.

Did you get the "Shiloh" article? I sent it to you. I sent it also to Paul Elder & Co. (New York branch) for their book of "Western Classics," and hope it will meet their need. They wanted something, and it seemed to me as good, with a little revision, as any of my stuff that I control. Do you think it would be wise to offer them for republication "In the Midst of Life"? It is now "out of print" and on my hands.

* * *

I'm glad of your commendation of my "Cosmopolitan" stuff. They don't give me much of a "show" — the editor doesn't love me personally as he should, and lets me do only enough to avert from himself the attention of Mr. Hearst and that gentleman's interference with the mutual admiration game as played in the "Cosmopolitan" office. As I'm rather fond of light work I'm not shrieking.

* * *

You don't speak of getting the book that I sent, "The Monk and the Hangman's Daughter"—new edition.'Tisn't as good as the old. * * *

I'm boating again. How I should like to put out my prow on Monterey Bay.   Sincerely yours,

                              AMBROSE BIERCE.

❦ ❦ ❦

The Army and
Navy Club,
Washington, D. C.,
June 8,
1907.

DEAR LORA,

Your letter, with the yerba buena and the spray of red-wood, came like a breeze from the hills. And the photographs are most pleasing. I note that Sloot's moustache is decently white at last, as becomes a fellow of his years. I dare say his hair is white too, but I can't see under his hat. And I think he never removes it. That backyard of yours is a wonder, but I sadly miss the appropriate ash-heaps, tin cans, old packing-boxes, and so forth. And that palm in front of the house — gracious, how she's grown! Well, it has been more than a day growing, and I've not watched it attentively.

I hope you'll have a good time in Yosemite, but Sloots is an idiot not to go with you — nineteen days is as long as anybody would want to stay there.

I saw a little of Phyllis Partington in New York. She told me much of you and seems to be fond of you. That is very intelligent of her, don't you think?

No, I shall not wait until I'm rich before visiting you. I've no intention of being rich, but do mean to visit you — some day. Probably when Grizzly has visited *me*. Love to you all.   AMBROSE BIERCE.

❦ ❦ ❦

Army and Navy Club,
Washington, D. C.,
June 25,
1907.

DEAR GEORGE,

                    * * *

So * * * showed you his article on me. He showed it to me also, and some of it amused me mightily, though I didn't tell him so. That picture of me as a grouchy and disappointed old man occupying the entire cave of Adullam is particularly humorous, and so poetic that I would not for the world "cut it out." * * * seems incapable (like a good many others) of estimating success in other terms than those of popularity. He gives a rather better clew to his own character than to mine. The old man is fairly well pleased with the way that he has played the game, and with his share of the stakes, thank'ee.

I note with satisfaction *your* satisfaction with my article on you and your poem. I'll correct the quotation about the "timid sapphires" — don't know how I happened to leave out the best part of it. But I left out the line about "harlot's blood" because I didn't (and don't) think a magazine would "stand for it" if I called the editor's attention to it. You don't know what magazines are if you haven't tested them. However, I'll try it on Chamberlain if you like. And I'll put in "twilight of the year" too.

* * *

It's pleasing to know that you've "cut out" your clerical work if you can live without it. Now for some great poetry! Carmel has a fascination for me too — because of your letters. If I did not fear illness — a return of my old complaint — I'd set out for it at once. I've nothing to do that would prevent — about two day's work a month. But I'd never set foot in San Francisco. Of all the Sodoms and Gomorrahs in our modern world it is the worst. There are not ten righteous (and courageous) men there. It needs another quake, another whiff of fire, and — more than all else — a steady tradewind of grapeshot. When * * * gets done blackguarding New York (as it deserves) and has shaken the dung of San Francisco from his feet I'm going to "sick him onto" that moral penal colony of the world. * * *

I've two "books" seeking existence in New York — the Howes book and some satires. Guess they are cocks that will not fight.　　　　　　　Sincerely yours,

AMBROSE BIERCE.

I was sixty-five yesterday.

❧ ❧ ❧

Washington, D. C.,
July 11,
1907.

DEAR GEORGE,

I've just finished reading proofs of my stuff about you and your poem. Chamberlain, as I apprised you, has it slated for September. But for that month also he has slated a longish spook story of mine, besides my regular stuff. Not seeing how he can run it all in one issue, I have asked him to run your poem (with my remarks) and hold the spook yarn till some other time. I *hope* he'll do so, but if he doesn't, don't think it my fault. An editor never does as one wants him to. I inserted in my article another quotation or two, and restored some lines that I had cut out of the quotations to save space.

It's grilling hot here — I envy you your Carmel.

Sincerely yours,

AMBROSE BIERCE.

❧ ❧ ❧

The Army and
Navy Club,
Washington, D. C.

DEAR GEORGE,

I guess several of your good letters are unanswered, as are many others of other correspondents. I've been gadding a good deal lately — to New York principally. When I want a royal good time I go to New York; and I get it.

* * *

As to Miller being "about the same age" as I, why, no. The rascal is long past seventy, although nine or ten years ago he wrote from Alaska that he was "in the middle fifties." I've known him for nearly thirty years and he can't fool me with his youthful airs and tales. May he live long and repent.

Thank you for taking the trouble to send Conan Doyle's opinion of me. No, it doesn't turn my head; I can show you dozens of "appreciations" from greater and more famous men. I return it to you corrected — as he really wrote it. Here it is:

"Praise from Sir Hugo is praise indeed." In "Through the Magic Door," an exceedingly able article on short stories that have interested him, Conan Doyle pays the following well-deserved tribute to Ambrose Bierce, whose wonderful short stories have so often been praised in these columns: "Talking of weird American stories, have you ever read any of the works of Ambrose Bierce? I have one of his books before me, 'In the Midst of Life.' This man (has)* had a flavor quite his own, and (is)* was a great artist. It is not cheerful reading, but it leaves its mark upon you, and that is the proof of good work."

Thank you also for the Jacobs story, which I will read. As a *humorist* he is no great thing.

I've not read your Bohemian play to a finish yet, * * *. By the way, I've always wondered why they did not "put on" Comus. Properly done it would be great woodland stuff. Read it with a view to that and see if I'm not right. And then persuade them to "stage it" next year.

I'm being awfully pressed to return to California. No San Francisco for me, but Carmel sounds good. For about how much could I get ground and build a bungalow — for one? That's a pretty indefinite question; but then the will to go is a little hazy at present. It consists, as yet, only of the element of desire. * * *

*Crossed out by A. B.

The "Cosmopolitan," with your poem, has not come to hand but is nearly due — I'm a little impatient — eager to see the particular kind of outrage Chamberlain's artist has wrought upon it. He (C.) asked for your address the other day; so he will doubtless send you a check.

* * *

Now please go to work at "Lilith"; it's bound to be great stuff, for you'll have to imagine it all. I'm sorry that anybody ever invented Lilith; it makes her too much of an historical character.

* * *

"The other half of the Devil's Dictionary" is in the fluid state — not even liquid. And so, doubtless, it will remain.

Sincerely yours,

AMBROSE BIERCE.

◦◦◦

The Army and Navy Club, Washington, D. C., September 7, 1907.

MY DEAR GEORGE,

I'm awfully glad that you don't mind Chamberlain's yellow nonsense in coupling Ella's name with yours. But when you read her natural opinion of your work you'll acquit her of complicity in the indignity. I'm sending a few things from Hearst's newspapers — written by the slangers, dialecters and platitudinarians of the staff, and by some of the swine among the readers.

Note the deliberate and repeated lying of Brisbane in quoting me as saying the "Wine" is "the greatest poem ever written in America." Note his dishonesty in confessing that he has commendatory letters, yet not publishing a single one of them. But the end is not yet — my inning is to come, in the magazine. Chamberlain (who professes an enthusiastic admiration of the poem) promises me a free hand in replying to these ignorant asses. If he does not give it to me I quit. I've writ a paragraph or two for the November number (too late now for the October) by way of warning them what they'll get when December comes. So you see you must patiently endure the befouling till then.

* * *

Did you notice in the last line of the "Wine" that I restored the word "smile" from your earlier draft of the verses? In one of your later (I don't remember if in the last) you had it "sigh." That was wrong; "smile" seems to me infinitely better as a definition of the poet's attitude toward his dreams. So, considering that I had a choice, I chose it. Hope you approve.

I am serious in wishing a place in Carmel as a port of refuge from the storms of age. I don't know that I shall ever live there, but should like to feel that I can if I want to. Next summer I hope to go out there and spy out the land, and if I then "have the price" (without sacrificing any of my favorite stocks) I shall buy. I don't care for the grub question — should like to try the simple life, for I have already two gouty finger points as a result of the other kind of life. (Of course if they all get that way I shan't mind, for I love uniformity.) Probably if I attempted to live in Carmel I should have asthma again, from which I have long been free. * * *

Sincerely yours,

AMBROSE BIERCE.

❧ ❧ ❧

MY DEAR MORROW,

Whether you "prosper" or not I'm glad you write instead of teaching. I have done a bit of teaching myself, but as the tuition was gratuitous I could pick my pupils; so it was a labor of love. I'm pretty well satisfied with the results.

Army and Navy Club, Washington, D. C., October 9, 1907.

No, I'm not "toiling" much now. I've written all I care to, and having a pretty easy berth (writing for The Cosmopolitan only, and having no connection with Mr. Hearst's newspapers) am content.

I have observed your story in Success, but as I never never (sic) read serials shall await its publication in covers before making a meal of it.

You seem to be living at the old place in Vallejo Street, so I judge that it was spared by the fire. I had some pretty good times in that house, not only with you and Mrs. Morrow (to whom my love, please) but with the dear Hogan girls. Poor Flodie! she is nearly a sole survivor now. I wonder if she ever thinks of us.

I hear from California frequently through a little group of interesting folk who foregather at Carmel — whither I shall perhaps stray some day and there leave my bones. Meantime, I am fairly happy here.

I wish you would add yourself to the Carmel crowd. You would be a congenial member of the gang and would find them worth while. You must know George Sterling: he is the high panjandrum and a gorgeously good fellow. Go get thee a bungalow at Carmel, which is indubitably the charmingest place in the State. As to San Francisco, with its labor-union government, its thieves and other impossibilities, I could not be drawn into it by a team of behemoths. But California — ah, I dare not permit myself to remember it. Yet this Eastern country is not without charm. And my health is good here, as it never was there. Nothing ails me but age, which brings its own cure.

God keep thee! — go and live at Carmel.

Sincerely yours,

AMBROSE BIERCE.

James D. Blake, Esq.,
Dear Sir:

It is a matter of no great importance to me, but the re- The Army and publication of the foolish books that you mention would Navy Club, Washington, D. C., not be agreeable to me. They have no kind of merit or October 29, interest. One of them, "The Fiend's Delight," was pub- 1907. lished against my protest; the utmost concession that the compiler and publisher (the late John Camden Hatten, London) would make was to let me edit his collection of my stuff and write a preface. You would pretty surely lose money on any of them.

If you care to republish anything of mine you would, I think, do better with "Black Beetles in Amber," or "Shapes of Clay." The former sold well, and the latter would, I think, have done equally well if the earthquake-and-fire had not destroyed it, including the plates. Nearly all of both books were sold in San Francisco, and the sold, as well as the unsold, copies — I mean the unsold copies of the latter — perished in the fire. There is much inquiry for them (mainly from those who lost them) and I am told that they bring fancy prices. You probably know about that better than I.

I should be glad to entertain proposals from you for their republication — in San Francisco — and should not be exacting as to royalties, and so forth.

But the other books are "youthful indiscretions" and are "better dead." Sincerely yours,   Ambrose Bierce.

꧁ ꧁ ꧁

Dear George,

* * *

Please send me a copy of the new edition of "The Testi- The Army and Navy Club, mony." I borrowed one of the first edition to give away, Washington, D. C., December 28, 1907.

and want to replace it. Did you add the "Wine" to it? I'd not leave off the indefinite article from the title of that; it seems to dignify the tipple by hinting that it was no ordinary tope. It may have been witch-fermented.

I don't "dislike" the line: "So terribly that brilliance shall enhance"; it seems merely less admirable than the others. Why didn't I tell you so? I could not tell you *all* I thought of the poem — for another example, how I loved the lines:

> "Where Dawn upon a pansy's breast hath laid
> A single tear, and *whence the wind hath flown*
> *And left a silence."*

* * *

I'm returning you, under another cover (as the ceremonial slangers say) some letters that have come to me and that I have answered. I have a lot more, most of them abusive, I guess, that I'll dig out later. But the most pleasing ones I can't send, for I sent them to Brisbane on his promise to publish them, which the liar did not, nor has he had the decency to return them. I'm hardly sorry, for it gave me good reason to call him a peasant and a beast of the field. I'm always grateful for the chance to prod somebody.

* * *

I detest the "limited edition" and "autograph copies" plan of publication, but for the sake of Howes, who has done a tremendous lot of good work on my book, have assented to Blake's proposal in all things and hope to be able to laugh at this brilliant example of the "irony of fate." I've refused to profit in any way by the book. I want Howes to "break even" for his labor.

By the way, Pollard and I had a good time in Galveston,

and on the way I took in some of my old battlefields. At Galveston they nearly killed me with hospitality — so nearly that Pollard fled. I returned via Key West and Florida.

You'll probably see Howes next Summer—I've persuaded him to go West and renounce the bookworm habit for some other folly. Be good to him; he is a capital fellow in his odd, amusing way.

I didn't know there was an American edition of "The Fiends' Delight." Who published it and when?

Congratulations on acceptance of "Tasso and Leonora." But I wouldn't do much in blank verse if I were you. It betrays you (somehow) into mere straightaway expression, and seems to repress in you the glorious abundance of imagery and metaphor that enriches your rhyme-work. This is not a criticism, particularly, of "Tasso," which is good enough for anybody, but — well, it's just *so.*

I'm not doing much. My stuff in the Cosmo. comes last, and when advertisements crowd some of it is left off. Most of it gets in later (for of course I don't replace it with more work) but it is sadly antiquated. My checks, though, are always up to date. Sincerely* yours, Ambrose Bierce.

*I can almost say "sinecurely."

ᔆ᎐ ᔆ᎐ ᔆ᎐

My dear George,

I have just come upon a letter of yours that I got at Galveston and (I fear) did not acknowledge. But I've written you since, so I fancy all is well.

The Army and Navy Club, Washington, D. C., January 19, 1908.

You mention that sonnet that Chamberlain asked for. You should not have let him have it — it was, as you say, the kind of stuff that magazines like. Nay, it was even better. But I wish you'd sent it elsewhere. You owed it to me not to let the Cosmopolitan's readers see anything of yours (for awhile, at least) that was less than *great*. Something as great as the sonnet that you sent to McClure's was what the circumstances called for.

"And strict concern of relativity" — O bother! that's not poetry. It's the slang of philosophy.

I am still awaiting my copy of the new "Testimony." That's why I'm scolding.   Sincerely yours,

AMBROSE BIERCE.

❦ ❦ ❦

The Army and
Navy Club,
Washington, D. C.,
April 18,
1908.

MY DEAR LORA,

I'm an age acknowledging your letter; but then you'd have been an age writing it if you had not done it for "Sloots." And the other day I had one from him, written in his own improper person.

I think it abominable that he and Carlt have to work so hard — at *their* age — and I quite agree with George Sterling that Carlt ought to go to Carmel and grow potatoes. I'd like to do that myself, but for the fact that so many objectionable persons frequent the place: * * *, * * * and the like. I'm hoping, however, that the ocean will swallow * * * and be unable to throw him up.

I trust you'll let Sloots "retire" at seventy, which is really quite well along in life toward the years of discretion and the age of consent. But when he is retired I know that he will bury himself in the redwoods and never look upon the face of man again. That, too, I should rather like to do myself — for a few months.

I've laid out a lot of work for myself this season, and doubt if I shall get to California, as I had hoped. So I shall never, never see you. But you might send me a photograph.

God be with you.   AMBROSE BIERCE.

N. B. If you follow the pages you'll be able to make *some* sense of this screed.

Washington, D. C.,
July 11,
1908.

MY DEAR GEORGE,

I am sorry to learn that you have not been able to break your commercial chains, since you wish to, though I don't at all know that they are bad for you. I've railed at mine all my life, but don't remember that I ever made any good use of leisure when I had it — unless the mere "having a good time" is such. I remember once writing that one's career, or usefulness, was about ended when one thought less about how best to do his work than about the hardship of having to do it. I might have said the hardship of having so little leisure to do it. As I grow older I see more and more clearly the advantages of disadvantage, the splendid urge of adverse conditions, the uplifting effect of repression. And I'm ashamed to note how little *I* profited by them. I wasn't the right kind, that is all; but I indulge the hope that *you* are.

No I don't think it of any use, your trying to keep * * * and me friends. But don't let that interfere with your regard for him if you have it. We are not required to share one another's feelings in such matters. I should not expect you to like my friends nor hate my enemies if they seemed to you different from what they seem to me; nor would I necessarily follow *your* lead. For example, I loathe your friend * * * and expect his safe return because the ocean will refuse to swallow him.

* * *

I congratulate you on the Gilder acceptance of your sonnet, and on publication of the "Tasso to Leonora." I don't think it your best work by much — don't think any of your blank verse as good as most of your rhyme — but it's not a thing to need apology.

Certainly, I shall be pleased to see Hopper. Give me his address, and when I go to New York — this month or the next — I'll look him up. I think well of Hopper and trust that he will not turn out to be an 'ist of some kind, as most writers and artists do. That is because they are good feelers and poor thinkers. It is the emotional element in them, not the logical, that makes them writers and artists. They have, as a rule, sensibility and no sense. Except the *big* fellows.

* * *

Neale has in hand already three volumes of the "Collected Works," and will have two more in about a month; and all (I hope) this year. I'm revising all the stuff and cutting it about a good deal, taking from one book stuff for another, and so forth. If Neale gets enough subscriptions he will put out all the ten volumes next year; if not I shall probably not be "here" to see the final one issued.

* * *

Glad you think better of my part in the Hunter-Hillquit "symposium." *I* think I did very well considering, first, that I didn't care a damn about the matter; second, that I knew nothing of the men I was to meet, nor what we were to talk about, whereas they came cocked and primed for the fray; and, third, that the whole scheme was to make a Socialist holiday at my expense. Of all 'ists the Socialist is perhaps the damnedest fool for (in this country) he is merely the cat that pulls chestnuts from the fire for the Anarchist. His part of the business is to talk away the country's attention while the Anarchist places the bomb. In some countries Socialism is clean, but not in this. And everywhere the Socialist is a dreamer and futilitarian.

But I guess I'll call a halt on this letter, the product of an idle hour in garrulous old age.

* * *

Sincerely yours,

AMBROSE BIERCE.

♥ ♥ ♥

MY DEAR MR. CAHILL,

Your note inquiring about "Ashes of the Beacon" interests me. You mention it as a "pamphlet." I have no knowledge of its having appeared otherwise than as an article in the Sunday edition of the "N. Y. American" — I do not recall the date. If it has been published as a pamphlet, or in any other form, separately — that is by itself — I should like "awfully" to know by whom, if *you* know.

The Army and Navy Club, Washington, D. C., August 7, 1908.

I should be pleased to send it to you—in the "American"— if I had a copy of the issue containing it, but I have not. It will be included in Vol. I of my "Collected Works," to be published by the Neale Publishing Company, N. Y. That volume will be published probably early next year.

But the work is to be in ten or twelve costly volumes, and sold by subscription only. That buries it fathoms deep so far as the public is concerned.

Regretting my inability to assist you, I am sincerely yours,

AMBROSE BIERCE.

♥ ♥ ♥

DEAR GEORGE,

I am amused by your attitude toward the spaced sonnet, and by the docility of Gilder. If I had been your editor I guess you'd have got back your sonnets. I never liked the space. If the work naturally divides itself into two parts, as it should, the space is needless; if not, it is worse than that. The space was the invention of printers of a comparatively

Washington, D. C., August 14, 1908.

recent period, neither Petrarch nor Dante (as Gilder points out) knew of it. Every magazine has its own *system* of printing, and Gilder's good-natured compliance with your wish, or rather demand, shows him to be a better fellow, though not a better poet, than I have thought him to be. As a victory of author over editor, the incident pleases.

I've not yet been in New York, but expect to go soon. I shall be glad to meet Hopper if he is there.

Thank you for the article from "Town Talk." It suggests this question: How many times, and covering a period of how many years, must one's unexplainable obscurity be pointed out to constitute fame? Not knowing, I am almost disposed to consider myself the most famous of authors. I have pretty nearly ceased to be "discovered," but my notoriety as an obscurian may be said to be worldwide and apparently everlasting.

The trouble, I fancy, is with our vocabulary — the lack of a word meaning something intermediate between "popular" and "obscure" — and the ignorance of writers as to the reading of readers. I seldom meet a person of education who is not acquainted with some of my work; my clipping bureau's bills were so heavy that I had to discontinue my patronage, and Blake tells me that he sells my books at one hundred dollars a set. Rather amusing all this to one so widely unknown.

I sometimes wonder what you think of Scheff's new book. Does it perform the promise of the others? In the dedicatory poem it seems to me that it does, and in some others. As a good Socialist you are bound to like *that* poem because of its political-economic-views. I like it despite them.

> "The dome of the Capitol roars
> With the shouts of the Caesars of crime"

is great poetry, but it is not true. I am rather familiar with what goes on in the Capitol — not through the muck-rakers, who pass a few days here "investigating," and then look into their pockets and write, but through years of personal observation and personal acquaintance with the men observed. There are no Caesars of crime, but about a dozen rascals, all told, mostly very small fellows; I can name them all. They are without power or influence enough to count in the scheme of legislation. The really dangerous and mischievous chaps are the demagogues, friends of the pee-pul. And they do all the "shouting." Compared with the Congress of our forefathers, the Congress of to-day is as a flock of angels to an executive body of the Western Federation of Miners.

When I showed the "dome" to * * * (who had been reading his own magazine) the tears came into his voice, and I guess his eyes, as he lamented the decay of civic virtue, "the treason of the Senate," and the rest of it. He was so affected that I hastened to brace him up with whiskey. He, too, was "squirming" about "other persons' troubles," and with about as good reason as you.

I think "the present system" is not "frightful." It is all right — a natural outgrowth of human needs, limitations and capacities, instinct with possibilities of growth in goodness, elastic, and progressively better. Why don't you study humanity as you do the suns — not from the viewpoint of time, but from that of eternity. The middle ages were yesterday, Rome and Greece the day before. The individual man is nothing, as a single star is nothing. If this earth were to take fire you would smile to think how little it mattered in the scheme of the universe; all the wailing of the egoist mob would not affect you. Then why do you squirm at the minute catastrophe of a few thousands or millions of pismires crushed under the wheels of evolution. Must the new heavens and the new earth of prophecy and science come in *your* little instant of life in order that you may not go howling and damning with Jack London up and down the earth that we happen to have? Nay, nay, read history to get the long, large view — to learn to think in centuries and cycles. Keep your eyes off your neighbors and fix them on the nations. What poetry we shall have when you get, and give us, The Testimony of the Races!

* * *

I peg away at compilation and revision. I'm cutting-about my stuff a good deal — changing things from one book to another, adding, subtracting and dividing. Five volumes are ready, and Neale is engaged in a "prospectus" which he says will make me blush. I'll send it to you when he has it ready.

Gertrude Atherton is sending me picture-postals of Berchtesgaden and other scenes of "The Monk and the Hangman's Daughter." She found all the places "exactly as described" — the lakes, mountains, St. Bartolomae, the cliff-meadow where the edelweiss grows, and so forth. The photographs are naturally very interesting to me.

Good night.

AMBROSE BIERCE.

Army and Navy Club, Washington, D. C., September 12, 1908.

MY DEAR MR. CAHILL,

Thank you for your good wishes for the "Collected Works" — an advertisement of which — with many blush-es! — I enclose.   Sincerely yours,

AMBROSE BIERCE.

P. S. — The "ad" is not sent in the hope that you will be so foolish as to subscribe — merely to "show" you. The "edition de luxe" business is not at all to my taste — I should prefer a popular edition at a possible price.

⚹ ⚹ ⚹

DEAR GEORGE,

Your letter has just been forwarded from Washington. I'm here for a few days only — "few days and full of trouble," as the Scripture hath it. The "trouble" is mainly owling, dining and booze. I'll not attempt an answer to your letter till I get home.

New York, November 6, 1908.

* * *

I'm going to read Hopper's book, and if it doesn't show him to be a * * * or a * * * I'll call on him. If it does I won't. I'm getting pretty particular in my old age; the muck-rakers, blood-boilers and little brothers-of-the-bad are not congenial.

By the way, why do you speak of my "caning" you. I did not suppose that *you* had joined the innumerable caravan of those who find something sarcastic or malicious in my good natured raillery in careless controversy. If I choose to smile in ink at your inconsistency in weeping for the woes of individual "others" — meaning other *humans* — while you, of course, don't give a damn for the thousands of lives that you crush out every time you set down your foot, or eat a berry, why shouldn't *I* do so? One can't always remember to stick to trifles, even in writing a letter. Put on your skin, old man, I may want to poke about with my finger again.   * * *

Sincerely yours,
AMBROSE BIERCE.

Washington, D. C.,
December 11,
1908.
DEAR GEORGE,

* * *

I'm still working at my book. Seven volumes are completed and I've read the proofs of Vol. I.

Your account of the "movement" to free the oppressed and downtrodden river from the tyranny of the sand-bar tickled me in my lonesome rib. Surely no colony of reformers ever engaged in a more characteristic crusade against the Established Order and Intolerable Conditions. I can almost hear you patting yourselves on your aching backs as you contemplated your encouraging success in beating Nature and promoting the Cause. I believe that if I'd been there my cold heart and indurated mind would have caught the contagion of the Great Reform. Anyhow, I should have appreciated the sunset which (characteristically) intervened in the interest of Things as They Are. I feel sure that whenever you Socialers shall have found a way to make the earth stop "turning over and over like a man in bed" (as Joaquin might say) you will accomplish all the reforms that you have at heart. All that you need is plenty of time—a few kalpas, more or less, of uninterrupted daylight. Meantime I await your new book with impatience and expectation.

I have photographs of my brother's shack in the redwoods and feel strongly drawn in that direction — since, as you fully infer, Carmel is barred. Probably, though, I shall continue in the complicated life of cities while I last.

Sincerely yours,

AMBROSE BIERCE.

Washington, D. C.,
January 9,
1909.
DEAR GEORGE,

I've been reading your book — re-reading most of it —

"every little while." I don't know that it is better than your first, but to say that it is as good is praise enough. You know what I like most in it, but there are some things that you *don't* know I like. For an example, "Night in Heaven." It Kipples a bit, but it is great. But I'm not going to bore you with a catalogue of titles. The book is *all* good. No, not (in my judgment) all, for it contains lines and words that I found objectionable in the manuscript, and time has not reconciled me to them. Your retention of them, shows, however, that you agree with me in thinking that you have passed your 'prentice period and need no further criticism. So I welcome them.

I take it that the cover design is Scheff's — perhaps because it is so good, for the little cuss is clever that way.

* * *

I rather like your defence of Jack London — not that I think it valid, but because I like loyalty to a friend whom one does not believe to be bad. (The "thick-and-thin" loyalty never commended itself to me; it is too dog-like.) I fail, however, to catch the note of penitence in London's narratives of his underlife, and my charge of literary stealing was not based on his primeval man book, "Before Adam."

As to * * *, as he is not more than a long-range or short-acquaintance friend of yours, I'll say that I would not believe him under oath on his deathbed. * * * The truth is, none of these howlers knows the difference between a million and a thousand nor between truth and falsehood. I could give you instances of their lying about matters here at the capital that would make even your hair stand on end. It is not only that they are all liars — they are mere children; they don't know anything and don't care to, nor, for prosperity in their specialties, need to. Veracity would be a disqualification; if they confined themselves to facts they would not get a hearing. * * * is the nastiest futilitarian of the gang.

It is not the purpose of these gentlemen that I find so very objectionable, but the foul means that they employ to accomplish it. I would be a good deal of a Socialist myself if they had not made the word (and the thing) stink.

Don't imagine that I'll not "enter Carmel" if I come out there. I'll visit you till you're sick of me. But I'd not *live* there and be "identified" with it, as the newspapers would say. I'm warned by Hawthorne and Brook Farm.

I'm still working — a little more leisurely — on my books. But I begin to feel the call of New York on the tympani of my blood globules. I must go there occasionally, or I should die of intellectual torpor. * * * "O Lord how long?" — this letter. O well, you need not give it the slightest attention; there's nothing, I think, that requires a reply, nor merits one.   Sincerely yours,

                                        AMBROSE BIERCE.

❧ ❧ ❧

Washington, D. C., DEAR GEORGE,
    March 6,   * * *
      1909.
Did you see Markham's review of the "Wine" in "The N. Y. American"? Pretty fair, but — if a metrical composition full of poetry is not a poem what is it? And I wonder what he calls Kubla Khan, which has a beginning but neither middle nor end. And how about The Faerie Queene for absence of "unity"? Guess I'll ask him.

Isn't it funny what happens to critics who would mark out meters and bounds for the Muse — denying the name "poem," for example, to a work because it is not like some other work, or like one that is in the minds of them?

I hope you are prosperous and happy and that I shall sometimes hear from you.

Howes writes me that the "Lone Hand" — Sydney — has been commending you.

Sincerely yours,

AMBROSE BIERCE.

❧ ❧ ❧

DEAR GEORGE,

I return the poems with a few random comments and suggestions. Washington, D. C., October 9, 1909.

I'm a little alarmed lest you take too seriously my preference of your rhyme to your blank — especially when I recall your "Music" and "The Spirit of Beauty." Perhaps I should have said only that you are not so *likely* to write well in blank. (I think always of "Tasso to Leonora," which I cannot learn to like.) Doubtless I have too great fondness for *great* lines — *your* great lines — and they occur less frequently in your blank verse than in your rhyme — most frequently in your quatrains, those of sonnets included. Don't swear off blank — except as you do drink — but study it more. It's "an hellish thing."

It looks as if I *might* go to California sooner than I had intended. My health has been wretched all summer. I need a sea voyage — one *via* Panama would be just the thing. So if the cool weather of autumn do not restore me I shall not await spring here. But I'm already somewhat better. If I had been at sea I should have escaped the Cook-Peary controversy. We talk nothing but arctic matters here — I enclose my contribution to its horrors.

I'm getting many a good lambasting for my book of essays.

Also a sop of honey now and then. It's all the same to me;
I don't worry about what my contemporaries think of me.
I made 'em think of *you* — that's glory enough for one.
And the squirrels in the public parks think me the finest
fellow in the world. They know what I have in every
pocket. Critics don't know that — nor nearly so much.

Advice to a young author: Cultivate the good opinion of
squirrels.   Sincerely yours,
                                          AMBROSE BIERCE.

ᘒᘐᐧ ᘒᘐᐧ ᘒᘐᐧ

Washington, D. C.,   DEAR GEORGE,
November 1,
1909.   European criticism of your *bête noir*, old Leopold, is entitled to attention; American (of him or any other king) is
not. It looks as if the wretch may be guilty of indifference.

In condemning as "revolutionary" the two-rhyme sestet,
I think I could not have been altogether solemn, for (1)
I'm something of a revolutionist myself regarding the sonnet, having frequently expressed the view that its accepted
forms — even the number of lines — were purely arbitrary;
(2) I find I've written several two-rhyme sestets myself,
and (3), like yours, my ear has difficulty in catching the
rhyme effect in a-b-c, a-b-c. The rhyme is delayed till the
end of the fourth line — as it is in the quatrain (not of the
sonnet) with unrhyming first and third lines — a form of
which I think all my multitude of verse supplies no example. I confess, though, that I did not know that Petrarch had made so frequent use of the 2-rhyme sestet.

I learn a little all the time; some of my old notions of
poetry seem to me now erroneous, even absurd. So I *may*
have been at one time a stickler for the "regular" three-
rhymer. Even now it pleases my ear well enow if the three
are not so arranged as to elude it. I'm sorry if I misled you.

You'd better 'fess up to your young friend, as I do to you — if I really was serious.

* * *

Of course I should be glad to see Dick, but don't expect to. They never come, and it has long been my habit to ignore every "declaration of intention."

I'm greatly pleased to know that you too like those lines of Markham that you quote from the "Wharf of Dreams." I've repeatedly told him that that sonnet was his greatest work, and those were its greatest lines. By the way, my young poet, Loveman, sends me a letter from Markham, asking for a poem or two for a book, "The Younger Choir," that he (M.) is editing. Loveman will be delighted by your good opinion of "Pierrot" — which still another magazine has returned to me. Guess I'll have to give it up.

I'm sending you a booklet on loose locutions. It is vilely gotten up — had to be so to sell for twenty-five cents, the price that I favored. I just noted down these things as I found them in my reading, or remembered them, until I had four hundred. Then I took about fifty from other books, and boiled down the needful damnation. Maybe I have done too much boiling down — making the stuff "thick and slab." If there is another edition I shall do a little bettering.

I should like some of those mussels, and, please God, shall help you cull them next summer. But the abalone — as a Christian comestible he is a stranger to me and the tooth o' me.

I think you have had some correspondence with my friend Howes of Galveston. Well, here he is "in his habit as he lives." Of the two figures in the picture Howes is the one on top.* Good night.   A. B.

*Howes was riding on a burro.

Washington, D. C.,
January 29,
1910.
DEAR GEORGE,

Here are your fine verses — I have been too busy to write to you before. In truth, I've worked harder now for more than a year than I ever shall again — and the work will bring me nor gain nor glory. Well, I shall take a rest pretty soon, partly in California. I thank you for the picture card. I have succumbed to the post-card fashion myself.

As to some points in your letter.

I've no recollection of advising young authors to "leave all heart and sentiment out of their work." If I did the context would probably show that it was because their time might better be given to perfect themselves in form, against the day when their hearts would be less wild and their sentiments truer. You know it has always been my belief that one cannot be trusted to feel until one has learned to think — and few youngsters have learned to do that. Was it not Dr. Holmes who advised a young writer to cut out every passage that he thought particularly good? He'd be sure to think the beautiful and sentimental passages the best, would he not? * * *

If you mean to write really "vituperative" sonnets (why sonnets?) let me tell you *one* secret of success — name your victim and his offense. To do otherwise is to fire blank cartridges — to waste your words in air — to club a vacuum. At least your satire must be so personally applicable that there can be no mistake as to the victim's identity. Otherwise he is no victim — just a spectator like all others. And that brings us to Watson. His caddishness consisted, not in satirizing a woman, which is legitimate, but, first, in doing so without sufficient reason, and, second, in saying orally (on the safe side of the Atlantic) what he apparently did not dare say in the verses. * * *

I'm enclosing something that will tickle you I hope —
"The Ballade of the Goodly Fere." The author's* father,
who is something in the Mint in Philadelphia, sent me several of his son's poems that were not good; but at last came
this — in manuscript, like the others. Before I could do
anything with it — meanwhile wearing out the paper and
the patience of my friends by reading it at them — the old
man asked it back rather peremptorily. I reluctantly sent
it, with a letter of high praise. The author had "placed" it
in London, where it has made a heap of talk.

It has plenty of faults besides its monotonous rhyme
scheme; but tell me what you think of it.

God willing, we shall eat Carmel mussels and abalones in
May or June. Sincerely yours,   AMBROSE BIERCE.

⚘ ⚘ ⚘

DEAR GEORGE,

My plan is to leave here before April first, pass a few days   Washington, D. C.,
in New York and then sail for Colon. If I find the canal   March 7,
work on the Isthmus interesting I may skip a steamer from   1910.
Panama to see it. I've no notion how long it will take to
reach San Francisco, and know nothing of the steamers
and their schedules on the Pacific side.

I shall of course want to see Grizzly first — that is to say,
he will naturally expect me to. But if you can pull him
down to Carmel about the time of my arrival (I shall write
you the date of my sailing from New York) I would gladly
come there. Carlt, whom I can see at once on arriving, can
tell me where he (Grizzly) is. * * *

I don't think you rightly value "The Goodly Fere." Of
course no ballad written to-day can be entirely good, for it
must be an imitation; it is now an unnatural form, whereas

*Ezra Pound.

it was once a natural one. We are no longer a primitive people, and a primitive people's forms and methods are not ours. Nevertheless, this seems to me an admirable ballad, as it is given a modern to write ballads. And I think you overlook the best line:

"The hounds of the crimson sky gave tongue."

The poem is complete as I sent it, and I think it stops right where and as it should —

"I ha' seen him eat o' the honey comb
Sin' they nailed him to the tree."

The current "Literary Digest" has some queer things about (and by) Pound, and "Current Literature" reprints the "Fere" with all the wrinkles ironed out of it — making a "capon priest" of it.

Fo' de Lawd's sake! don't apologise for not subscribing for my "Works." If you did subscribe I should suspect that you were "no friend o' mine" — it would remove you from that gang and put you in a class by yourself. Surely you can not think I care who buys or does not buy my books. The man who expects anything more than lip-service from his friends is a very young man. There are, for example, a half-dozen Californians (all loud admirers of Ambrose Bierce) editing magazines and newspapers here in the East. Every man Jack of them has turned me down. They will do everything for me but enable me to live. Friends be damned!—strangers are the chaps for me.

* * *

I've given away my beautiful sailing canoe and shall never again live a life on the ocean wave — unless you have boats at Carmel. Sincerely yours,   AMBROSE BIERCE.

DEAR GEORGE,

Here's a letter from Loveman, with a kindly reference to you — that's why I send it.

Washington, D. C., Easter Sunday.

I'm to pull out of here next Wednesday, the 30th, but don't know just when I shall sail from New York — apparently when there are no more dinners to eat in that town and no more friends to visit. May God in His infinite mercy lessen the number of both. I should get into your neck o' woods early in May. Till then God be with you instead.

AMBROSE BIERCE.

Easter Sunday.
[Why couldn't He stay put?]

◖◗ ◖◗ ◖◗

DEAR GEORGE,

I'm "all packed up," even my pens; for to-morrow I go to New York — whence I shall write you before embarking.

Washington, D. C., March 29, 1910.

Neale seems pleased by your "permission to print," as Congressmen say who can't make a speech yet want one in the Record, for home consumption.

Sincerely,

AMBROSE BIERCE.

◖◗ ◖◗ ◖◗

DEAR GEORGE,

You will probably have learned of my arrival — this is my first leisure to apprise you.

Guerneville, Cal., May 24, 1910.

I took Carlt and Lora and came directly up here — where we all hope to see you before I see Carmel. Lora remains here for the week, perhaps longer, and Carlt is to come up again on Saturday. Of course you do not need an invitation to come whenever you feel like it.

I had a pleasant enough voyage and have pretty nearly

got the "slosh" of the sea out of my ears and its heave out of my bones.

A bushel of letters awaits attention, besides a pair of lizards that I have undertaken to domesticate. So good morning.   Sincerely yours,

AMBROSE BIERCE.

✄ ✄ ✄

The Key Route Inn,   DEAR GEORGE,
Oakland,
June 25,   You'll observe that I acted on your suggestion, and am
1910.   "here."

Your little sisters are most gracious to me, despite my candid confession that I extorted your note of introduction by violence and intimidation.

Baloo* and his cubs went on to Guerneville the day of their return from Carmel. But I saw them.

I'm deep in work, and shall be for a few weeks; then I shall be off to Carmel for a lungful of sea air and a bellyful of abalones and mussels.

I suppose you'll be going to the Midsummer Jinks. Fail not to stop over here — I don't feel that I have really seen you yet.

With best regards to Carrie.

Sincerely yours,

AMBROSE BIERCE.

✄ ✄ ✄

The Laguna Vista,   DEAR GEORGE,
Oakland,
Sunday, July 24,   Supposing you to have gone home, I write to send the
1910.   poem. Of course it is a good poem. But I begin to want to hear your larger voice again. I want to see you standing tall on the heights — above the flower-belt and the bird-belt. I want to hear,

*Albert Bierce.

"like Ocean on a western beach,
The surge and thunder of the Odyssey,"

as you *Odyssate*.

I *think* I met that dog * * * to-day, and as it was a choice between kicking him and avoiding him I chose the more prudent course.

I've not seen your little sisters — they seem to have tired of me. Why not? — I have tired of myself.

Fail not to let me know when to expect you for the Guerneville trip. * * *

Sincerely yours,

AMBROSE BIERCE.

❧ ❧ ❧

I go back to the Inn on Saturday.

DEAR GEORGE,

It is long since I read the Book of Job, but if I thought it better than your addition to it I should not sleep until I had read it again — and again. Such a superb Who's Who in the Universe! Not a Homeric hero in the imminence of a personal encounter ever did so fine bragging. I hope you will let it into your next book, if only to show that the "inspired" scribes of the Old Testament are not immatchable by modern genius. You know the Jews regard them, not as prophets, in our sense, but merely as poets — and the Jews ought to know something of their own literature.

I fear I shall not be able to go to Carmel while you're a widow — I've tangled myself up with engagements again. Moreover, I'm just back from the St. Helena cemetery, and for a few days shall be too blue for companionship.

"Shifted" is better, I think (in poetry) than "joggled."

You say you "don't like working." Then write a short

The Laguna Vista, October 20, 1910.

story. That's work, but you'd like it — or so I think. Poetry is the highest of arts, but why be a specialist?

Sincerely yours,

AMBROSE BIERCE.

෨෧ ෨෧ ෨෧

Army and Navy Club,
Washington, D. C.,
November 11,
1910.

DEAR LORA,

It is nice to hear from you and learn that despite my rude and intolerant ways you manage to slip in a little affection for me — you and the rest of the folk. And really I think I left a little piece of my heart out there — mostly in Berkeley. It is funny, by the way, that in falling out of love with most of my old sweethearts and semi-sweethearts I should fall *in* love with my own niece. It is positively scandalous!

I return Sloot's letter. It gave me a bit of a shock to have him say that he would probably never see me again. Of course that is true, but I had not thought of it just that way — had not permitted myself to, I suppose. And, after all, if things go as I'm hoping they will, Montesano will take me in again some day before he seems likely to leave it. We four may see the Grand Cañon together yet. I'd like to lay my bones thereabout.

The garments that you persuaded me were mine are not. They are probably Sterling's, and he has probably damned me for stealing them. I don't care; he has no right to dress like the "filthy rich." Hasn't he any "class consciousness"? However, I am going to send them back to you by express. I'll mail you the paid receipt; so don't pay the charge that the company is sure to make. They charged me again for the two packages that you paid for, and got away with the money from the Secretary of my club, where they were delivered. I had to get it back from the delivery man at the cannon's mouth — 34 calibre.

With love to Carlt and Sloots,

Affectionately yours,

Ambrose.

❦ ❦ ❦

Dear Lora,

* * *

You asked me about the relative interest of Yosemite and the Grand Cañon. It is not easy to compare them, they are so different. In Yosemite only the magnitudes are unfamiliar; in the Cañon nothing is familiar — at least, nothing would be familiar to you, though I have seen something like it on the upper Yellowstone. The "color scheme" is astounding — almost incredible, as is the "architecture." As to magnitudes, Yosemite is nowhere. From points on the rim of the Cañon you can see fifty, maybe a hundred, miles of it. And it is never twice alike. Nobody can describe it. Of course you must see it sometime. I wish our Yosemite party could meet there, but probably we never will; it is a long way from here, and not quite next door to Berkeley and Carmel.

The Army and Navy Club, Washington, D. C., November 14, 1910.

I've just got settled in my same old tenement house, the Olympia, but the club is my best address.

* * *

Affectionately,

Ambrose.

❦ ❦ ❦

Dear Lora,

Thank you very much for the work that you are doing for me in photography and china. I know it is great work. But take your time about it.

Washington, D. C., November 29, 1910.

I hope you all had a good Thanksgiving at Upshack. (That is my name for Sloots' place. It will be understood by anyone that has walked to it from Montesano, carrying a basket of grub on a hot day.)

I trust Sterling got his waistcoat and trousers in time to appear at his uncle's dinner in other outer garments than a steelpen coat. * * * I am glad you like (or like to have) the books. You would have had all my books when published if I had supposed that you cared for them, or even knew about them. I am now encouraged to hope that some day you and Carlt and Sloots may be given the light to see the truth at the heart of my "views" (which I have expounded for half a century) and will cease to ally yourselves with what is most hateful to me, socially and politically. I shall then feel (in my grave) that perhaps, after all, I knew how to write. Meantime, run after your false fool gods until you are tired; I shall not believe that your hearts are really in the chase, for they are pretty good hearts, and those of your gods are nests of nastiness and heavens of hate.

Now I feel better, and shall drink a toddy to the tardy time when those whom I love shall not think me a perverted intelligence; when they shall not affirm my intellect and despise its work — confess my superior understanding and condemn all its fundamental conclusions. Then we will be a happy family — you and Carlt in the flesh and Sloots and I in our bones.

* * *

My health is excellent in this other and better world than California.

God bless you.   AMBROSE.

❧ ❧ ❧

Washington, D. C.,   DEAR CARLT,
December 22,
1910.   You had indeed "something worth writing about" — not

only the effect of the impenitent mushroom, but the final and disastrous overthrow of that ancient superstition, Sloots' infallibility as a mushroomer. As I had expected to be at that dinner, I suppose I should think myself to have had "a narrow escape." Still, I wish I could have taken my chance with the rest of you.

How would you like three weeks of nipping cold weather, with a foot of snow? That's what has been going on here. Say, tell Sloots that the front footprints of a rabbit-track

are made by the animal's hind feet, straddling his forelegs. Could he have learned that important fact in California, except by hearsay? Observe (therefore) the superiority of this climate.   * * *   Ambrose.

Dear Lora,

I have just received a very affectionate letter from * * * Washington, D. C., and now know that I did her an injustice in what I care- January 26, lessly wrote to you about her incivility to me after I had 1911. left her. It is plain that she did not mean to be uncivil in what she wrote me on a postal card which I did not look at until I was in the train; she just "didn't know any better." So I have restored her to favor, and hope that you will con- sider my unkind remarks about her as unwritten. Guess I'm addicted to going off at half-cock anyhow.

Affectionately,

Ambrose.

Dear Lora,

I have the Yosemite book, and Miss Christiansen has the Washington, D. C. Mandarin coat. I thank you very much. The pictures are February 3, beautiful, but of them all I prefer that of Nanny bending 1911.

over the stove. True, the face is not visible, but it looks like you all over.

I'm filling out the book with views of the Grand Cañon, so as to have my scenic treasures all together. Also I'm trying to get for you a certain book of Cañon pictures, which I neglected to obtain when there. You will like it — if I get it.

Sometime when you have nothing better to do — don't be in a hurry about it — will you go out to Mountain View cemetery with your camera and take a picture of the grave of Elizabeth (Lily) Walsh, the little deaf mute that I told you of? I think the man in the office will locate it for you. It is in the Catholic part of the cemetery — St. Mary's. The name Lily Walsh is on the beveled top of the headstone which is shaped like this:

You remember I was going to take you there, but never found the time.

Miss Christiansen says she is writing, or has written you. I think the coat very pretty.   Affectionately,

AMBROSE.

❧ ❧ ❧

Washington, D. C.,
February 15,
1911. DEAR GEORGE,

As to the "form of address." A man passing another was halted by the words: "You dirty dog!" Turning to the speaker, he bowed coldly and said: "Smith is my name, sir." *My* name is Bierce, and I find, on reflection, that I like best those who call me just that. If my christen name were George I'd want to be called *that*; but "Ambrose" is fit only for mouths of women — in which it sounds fairly well.

How are you my master? I never read one of your poems

without learning something, though not, alas, how to make one.

Don't worry about "Lilith"; it will work out all right. As to the characters not seeming alive, I've always fancied the men and women of antiquity — particularly the kings, and great ones generally — should not be too flesh-and-bloody, like the "persons whom one meets." A little coldness and strangeness is very becoming to them. I like them to *stalk*, like the ghosts that they are — our modern passioning seems a bit anachronous in them. Maybe I'm wrong, but I'm sure you will understand and have some sympathy with the error.

Hudson Maxim takes medicine without biting the spoon. He had a dose from me and swallowed it smiling. I too gave him some citations of great poetry that is outside the confines of his "definition" — poetry in which are no tropes at all. He seems to lack the *feel* of poetry. He even spoils some of the "great lines" by not including enough of the context. As to his "improvements," fancy his preference for "the fiercest spirit of *the warrior host*" to "the fiercest spirit *that fought in Heaven*"! O my!

Yes, Conrad told me the tale of his rescue by you. He gave me the impression of hanging in the sky above billows unthinkably huge and rocks inconceivably hard.

* * *

Of course I could not but be pleased by your inclusion of that sonnet on me in your book. And, by the way, I'm including in my tenth volume my *Cosmopolitan* article on the "Wine" and my end of the controversy about it. All the volumes of the set are to be out by June, saith the publisher. He is certainly half-killing me with proofs — mountains of proofs! * * *

Yes, you'll doubtless have a recruit in Carlt for your Socialist menagerie — if he is not already a veteran exhibit. Your "party" is recruited from among sore-heads only. There are some twenty-five thousand of them (sore-heads) in this neck o' woods — all disloyal — all growling at the Government which feeds and clothes them twice as well as they could feed and clothe themselves in private employment. They move Heaven and Earth to get in, and they never resign — just "take it out" in abusing the Government. If I had my way nobody should remain in the civil service more than five years — at the end of that period all are disloyal. Not one of them cares a rap for the good of the service or the country — as we soldiers used to do on thirteen dollars a month (with starvation, disease and death thrown in). Their grievance is that the Government does not undertake to maintain them in the style to which they choose to accustom themselves. They fix their standard of living just a little higher than they can afford, and would do so no matter what salary they got, as all salary-persons invariably do. Then they damn their employer for not enabling them to live up to it.

If they can do better "outside" why don't they go outside and do so; if they can't (which means that they are getting more than they are worth) what are they complaining about?

What this country needs — what every country needs occasionally — is a good hard bloody war to revive the vice of patriotism on which its existence as a nation depends. Meantime, you socialers, anarchists and other sentimentaliters and futilitarians will find the civil-service your best recruiting ground, for it is the Land of Reasonless Discontent. I yearn for the strong-handed Dictator who will swat

you all on the mouths o' you till you are "heard to cease."
Until then — How? (drinking.) Yours sincerely,

AMBROSE BIERCE.

૭ૄ ૭ૄ ૭ૄ

DEAR LORA,

Every evening coffee is made for me in my rooms, but I
have not yet ventured to take it from *your* cup for fear of
an accident to the cup. Some of the women in this house
are stark, staring mad about that cup and saucer, and the
plate.

Washington, D. C.,
February 19,
1911.

I am very sorry Carlt finds his position in the civil service
so intolerable. If he can do better outside he should resign.
If he can't, why, that means that the Government is doing
better for him than he can do for himself, and you are not
justified in your little tirade about the oppression of "the
masses." "The masses" have been unprosperous from time
immemorial, and always will be. A very simple way to escape that condition (and the *only* way) is to elevate oneself
out of that incapable class.

You write like an anarchist and say that if you were a
man you'd *be* one. I should be sorry to believe that, for I
should lose a very charming niece, and you a most worthy
uncle.

You say that Carlt and Grizzly are not Socialists. Does
that mean that *they* are anarchists? I draw the line at
anarchists, and would put them all to death if I lawfully
could.

But I fancy your intemperate words are just the babbling
of a thoughtless girl. In any case you ought to know from
my work in literature that I am not the person to whom to
address them. I carry my convictions into my life and conduct, into my friendships, affections and all my relations

with my fellow creatures. So I think it would be more considerate to leave out of your letters to *me* some things that you may have in mind. Write them to others.

My own references to socialism, and the like, have been jocular — I did not think you perverted "enough to hurt," though I consider your intellectual environment a mighty bad one. As to such matters in future let us make a treaty of silence. Affectionately,   AMBROSE.

❧ ❧ ❧

The Army and
Navy Club,
Washington, D. C.,
March 1,
1911.
MY DEAR RUTH,

It is pleasant to know that the family Robertson is "seeing things" and enjoying them. I hate travel, but find it delightful when done by you, instead of me. Believe me, I have had great pleasure in following you by your trail of words, as in the sport known as the "paper chase."

And now about the little story. Your refusal to let your father amend it is no doubt dreadfully insubordinate, but I brave his wrath by approval. It is *your* work that I want to see, not anybody's else. I've a profound respect for your father's talent: as a litérateur, he is the best physician that I know; but he must not be coaching my pupil, or he and I (as Mark Twain said of Mrs. Astor) "will have a falling out."

The story is not a story. It is not narrative, and nothing occurs. It is a record of mental mutations — of spiritual vicissitudes — states of mind. That is the most difficult thing that you could have attempted. It can be done acceptably by genius and the skill that comes of practice, as can anything. You are not quite equal to it — yet. You have done it better than I could have done it at your age, but not altogether well; as doubtless you did not expect to do it. It would be better to confine yourself at present to simple narrative. Write of something done, not of something thought and felt, except incidentally. I'm sure it is in you to do great work, but in this writing trade, as in other matters, excellence is to be attained no otherwise than by beginning at the beginning — the simple at first, then the complex and difficult. You can not go up a mountain by a leap at the peak.

I'm retaining your little sketch till your return, for you can do nothing with it — nor can I. If it had been written — preferably typewritten — with wide lines and margins I could do something *to* it. Maybe when I get the time I shall; at present I am swamped with "proofs" and two volumes behind the printers. If I knew that I should *see* you and talk it over I should rewrite it and (original in hand) point out the reasons for each alteration — you would see them quickly enough when shown. Maybe you will all come this way.

You are *very* deficient in spelling. I hope that is not incurable, though some persons — clever ones, too — never do learn to spell correctly. You will have to learn it from your reading — noting carefully all but the most familiar words.

You have "pet" words — nearly all of us have. One of yours is "flickering." Addiction to certain words is an "upsetting sin" most difficult to overcome. Try to overcome it by cutting them out where they seem most felicitous.

By the way, your "hero," as you describe him, would not have been accessible to all those spiritual impressions — it is *you* to whom they come. And that confirms my judgment of your imagination. Imagination is nine parts of the writing trade. With enough of *that* all things are possible; but it is the other things that require the hard work, the incessant study, the tireless seeking, the indomitable will.

It is no "pic-nic," this business of writing, believe me. Success comes by favor of the gods, yes; but O the days and nights that you must pass before their altars, prostrate and imploring! They are exacting — the gods; years and years of service you must give in the temple. If you are prepared to do this go on to your reward. If not, you can not too quickly throw away the pen and — well, marry, for example.

"Drink deep or taste not the Pierian spring."

My vote is that you persevere.

With cordial regards to all good Robertsons — I think there are no others — I am most sincerely your friend,

AMBROSE BIERCE.

❧ ❧ ❧

Washington, D. C.,
April 20,
1911.

DEAR LORA,

Thank you for the pictures of the Sloots fire-place and "Joe Gans." I can fancy myself cooking a steak in the one, and the other eating one better cooked.

I'm glad I've given you the Grand Cañon fever, for I hope to revisit the place next summer, and perhaps our Yosemite bunch can meet me there. My outing this season will be in Broadway in little old New York. That is not as good as Monte Sano, but the best that I can do.

You must have had a good time with the Sterlings, and doubtless you all suffered from overfeeding.

Carlt's action in denuding the shaggy pelt of his hands meets with my highest commendation, but you'd better look out. It may mean that he has a girl — a Jewess descended from Jacob, with an hereditary antipathy to anything like Esau. Carlt was an Esaurian.

You'll have to overlook some bad errors in Vol. V of the C. W. I did not have the page proofs. Some of the verses are unintelligible. That's the penalty for philandering in California instead of sticking to my work.

* * *

Affectionately,

AMBROSE.

ॐ ॐ ॐ

DEAR GEORGE,

I've been having noctes ambrosianæ with "The House of Orchids," though truly it came untimely, for I've not yet done reading your other books. Don't crowd the dancers, please. I don't know (and you don't care) what poem in it I like best, but I get as much delight out of these lines as out of any:

Washington, D. C., April 28, 1911.

> "Such flowers pale as are
> Worn by the goddess of a distant star—
> Before whose holy eyes
> Beauty and evening meet."

And — but what's the use? I can't quote the entire book.

I'm glad you did see your way to make "Memory" a female.

To Hades with Bonnet's chatter of gems and jewels — among the minor poetic properties they are better (to my taste) than flowers. By the way, I wonder what "lightness" Bonnet found in the "Apothecary" verses. They seem to me very serious.

Rereading and rereading of the Job confirm my first opinion of it. I find only one "bad break" in it — and that not inconsistent with God's poetry in the real Job: "ropes of adamant." A rope of stone is imperfectly conceivable — is, in truth, mixed metaphor.

I think it was a mistake for you to expound to Ned Hamilton, or anybody, how you wrote the "Forty-third Chapter," or anything. When an author explains his methods of composition he cannot expect to be taken seriously. Nine writers in ten wish to have it thought that they "dash off" things. Nobody believes it, and the judicious would be sorry to believe it. Maybe you do, but I guess you work hard and honestly enough over the sketch "dashed off." If you don't — do.   * * *

With love to Carrie, I will leave you to your sea-gardens and abalones. Sincerely yours,   AMBROSE BIERCE.

I'm off to Broadway next week for a season of old-gentle-manly revelry.

᠀᠑ ᠀᠑ ᠀᠑

Washington, D. C., May 2, 1911.

DEAR GEORGE,

In packing (I'm going to New York) I find this "Tidal" typoscript, and fear that I was to have returned it. Pray God it was not my neglect to do so that kept it out of the book. But if not, what did keep it out? Maybe the fact that it requires in the reader an uncommon acquaintance with the Scriptures.

If Robertson publishes any more books for you don't let him use "silver" leaf on the cover. It is not silver, cannot be neatly put on, and will come off. The "Wine" book is incomparably better and more tasteful than either of the others. By the way, I stick to my liking for Scheff's little vignette on the "Wine."

In "Duandon" you — *you*, Poet of the Heavens! — come perilously near to qualifying yourself for "mention" in a certain essay of mine on the blunders of writers and artists in matters lunar. You must have observed that imme-diately after the full o' the moon the light of that orb takes on a redness, and when it rises after dark is hardly a "towering glory," nor a "frozen splendor." Its "web" is not "silver." In truth, the gibbous moon, rising, has something of menace in its suggestion. Even twenty-four (or rather twenty-five) hours "after the full" this change in the quality and quantity of its light is very marked. I don't know what causes the sudden alteration, but it has always impressed me.

I feel a little like signing this criticism "Gradgrind," but anyhow it may amuse you.

Do you mind squandering ten cents and a postage stamp on me? I want a copy of *Town Talk* — the one in which you are a "Varied Type."

I don't know much of some of your poets mentioned in that article, but could wish that you had said a word about Edith Thomas. Thank you for your too generous mention of me — who brought you so much vilification!

Sincerely yours,
AMBROSE BIERCE.

꙾ ꙾ ꙾

MY DEAR RUTH,

You are a faithful correspondent; I have your postals from Athens and Syracuse, and now the letter from Rome. The Benares sketch was duly received, and I wrote you about it to the address that you gave — Cairo, I think. As you will doubtless receive my letter in due time I will not now repeat it — further than to say that I liked it. If it had been accompanied by a few photographs (indispensable now to such articles) I should have tried to get it into some magazine. True, Benares, like all other Asiatic and European cities, is pretty familiar to even the "general reader," but the sketch had something of the writer's personality in it — the main factor in all good writing, as in all forms of art.

Washington, D. C., May 29, 1911.

May I tell you what you already know — that you are deficient in spelling and punctuation? It is worth while to know these things — and all things that you can acquire. Some persons can not acquire orthography, and I don't wonder, but every page of every good book is a lesson in punctuation. One's punctuation is a necessary part of one's style; you cannot attain to precision if you leave that matter to editors and printers.

You ask if "stories" must have action. The name "story" is preferably used of narrative, not reflection nor mental analysis. The "psychological novel" is in great vogue just now, for example — the adventures of the mind, it might be called — but it requires a profounder knowledge of life and character than is possible to a young girl of whatever talent; and the psychological "short story" is even more difficult. Keep to narrative and simple description for a few years, until your wings have grown. These descriptions of foreign places that you write me are good practice. You are not likely to tell me much that I do not know, nor is that necessary; but your way of telling what I do know is sometimes very interesting as a study of *you*. So write me all you will, and if you would like the letters as a record of your travels you shall have them back; I am preserving them.

I judge from your letter that your father went straight through without bothering about me. Maybe I should not have seen him anyhow, for I was away from Washington for nearly a month.

Please give my love to your mother and sister, whom, of course, you are to bring here. I shall not forgive you if you do not.

Yes, I wish that you lived nearer to me, so that we could go over your work together. I could help you more in a few weeks *that* way than in years *this* way. God never does anything just right. Sincerely yours,   AMBROSE BIERCE.

❧❧ ❧❧ ❧❧

DEAR GEORGE,

Thank you for that Times "review." It is a trifle less malicious than usual — regarding *me*, that is all. My publisher, Neale, who was here last evening, is about "taking action" against that concern for infringement of his copyright in my little book, "Write It Right." The wretches have been serving it up to their readers for several weeks as the work of a woman named Learned. Repeatedly she uses my very words — whole passages of them. They refused even to confess the misdeeds of their contributrix, and persist in their sin. So they will have to fight.

Washington, D. C.,
July 31,
1911.

* * * I have never been hard on women whose hearts go with their admiration, and whose bodies follow their hearts — I don't mean that the latter was the case in this instance. Nor am I very exacting as to the morality of my men friends. I would not myself take another man's woman, any more than I would take his purse. Nor, I trust, would I seduce the daughter or sister of a friend, nor any maid whom it would at all damage — and as to *that* there is no hard and fast rule.

* * *

A fine fellow, I, to be casting the first stone, or the one-hundredth, at a lovelorn woman, weak or strong! By the way, I should not believe in the love of a strong one, wife, widow or maid.

It looks as if I may get to Sag Harbor for a week or so in the middle of the month. It is really not a question of expense, but Neale has blocked out a lot of work for me. He wants two more volumes — even five more if I'll make 'em.

Guess I'll give him two. In a week or so I shall be able to say whether I can go Sagharboring. If so, I think we should have a night in New York first, no? You could motor-boat up and back.   Sincerely yours,

AMBROSE BIERCE.*

❧ ❧ ❧

Washington, D. C.,
Monday,
August 7,
1911.
DEAR GEORGE,

In one of your letters you were good enough to promise me a motorboat trip from New York to Sag Harbor. I can think of few things more delightful than navigating in a motorboat the sea that I used to navigate in an open canoe; it will seem like Progress. So if you are still in that mind please write me what day *after Saturday next* you can meet me in New York and I'll be there. I should prefer that you come the day before the voyage and dine with me that evening.

I always stay at the Hotel Navarre, 7th avenue and 38th street. If unable to get in there I'll leave my address there. Or, tell me where *you* will be.

Sincerely yours,

AMBROSE BIERCE.

If the motorboat plan is not practicable let me know and I'll go by train or steamer; it will not greatly matter. A. B.

❧ ❧ ❧

Washington, D. C.,
Tuesday,
August 8,
1911.
DEAR GEORGE,

* * *

Kindly convey to young Smith of Auburn my felicitations on his admirable "Ode to the Abyss"—a large theme, treated with dignity and power. It has many striking passages—such, for example, as "The Romes of ruined spheres." I'm conscious of my sin against the rhetoricians

*Addressed to George Sterling at Sag Harbor, Long Island.

in liking that, for it jolts the reader out of the Abyss and
back to earth. Moreover, it is a metaphor which belittles,
instead of dignifying. But I like it.

He is evidently a student of George Sterling, and being in
the formative stage, cannot — why should he? — conceal
the fact.

My love to all good Californians of the Sag Harbor colony.

Sincerely yours,

AMBROSE BIERCE.

ᴓ ᴓ ᴓ

DEAR GEORGE,

It is good to know that you are again happy — that is to Washington, D. C.,
November 16,
1911.
say, you are in Carmel. For your *future* happiness (if suc-
cess and a certain rounding off of your corners would bring
it, as I think) I could wish you in New York or thereabout.
As the Scripture hath it: "It is not good for a man to be in
Carmel" — *Revised Inversion.* I note that at the late elec-
tion California damned herself to a still lower degradation
and is now unfit for a white man to live in. Initiative, ref-
erendum, recall, employers' liability,woman suffrage —yah!

* * *

But you are not to take too seriously my dislike of* * * *
I like him personally very well; he talks like a normal human being. It is only that damned book of his. He was here
and came out to my tenement a few evenings ago, finding
me in bed and helpless from lumbago, as I was for weeks. I
am now able to sit up and take notice, and there are even
fears for my recovery. My enemies would say, as Byron
said of Lady B., I am becoming "dangerously well again."

* * *

As to harlots, there are not ten in a hundred that are such

*Excised by G. S.

for any other reason than that they wanted to be. Their exculpatory stories are mostly lies of magnitude.

Sloots writes me that he will perhaps "walk over" from the mine to Yosemite next summer. I can't get there much before July first, but if there is plenty of snow in the mountains next winter the valley should be visitable then. Later, I hope to beguest myself for a few days at the Pine Inn, Carmel. Tell it not to the Point Lobos mussel!

My love to Carrie.   Sincerely yours,

AMBROSE BIERCE.

🙠 🙠 🙠

Washington, D. C.,
December 27,
1911. DEAR GEORGE,

As you do not give me that lady's address I infer that you no longer care to have me meet her—which is a relief to me.

* * *

Yes, I'm a bit broken up by the death of Pollard, whose body I assisted to burn. He lost his mind, was paralyzed, had his head cut open by the surgeons, and his sufferings were unspeakable. Had he lived he would have been an idiot; so it is all right —

"But O, the difference to me!"

If you don't think him pretty bright read any of his last three books, "Their Day in Court," "Masks and Minstrels," and "Vagabond Journeys." He did not see the last one — Neale brought down copies of it when he came to Baltimore to attend the funeral.

I'm hoping that if Carlt and Lora go to Wagner's mine and we go to Yosemite, Lora, at least, will come to us out there. We shall need her, though Carrie will find that Misses C. and S. will be "no deadheads in the enterprise" — to quote a political phrase of long ago. As to me, I shall leave my ten-pounds-each books at home and, like St. Jerome, who never traveled with other baggage than a skull, be "flying light."

My love to Carrie.   Sincerely,
                                      AMBROSE BIERCE.

❧ ❧ ❧

DEAR LORA,

It is good to hear from you again, even if I did have to give you a hint that I badly needed a letter. Washington, D. C., January 5, 1912.

I am glad that you are going to the mine (if you go) — though Berkeley and Oakland will not be the same without you. And where can I have my mail forwarded? — and be permitted to climb in at the window to get it. As to pot-steaks, toddies, and the like, I shall simply swear off eating and drinking.

If Carlt is a "game sport," and does not require "a dead-sure thing," the mining gamble is the best bet for him. Anything to get out of that deadening, hopeless grind, the "Government service." It kills a man's self-respect, atrophies his powers, unfits him for anything, tempts him to improvidence and then turns him out to starve.

It is pleasant to know that there is a hope of meeting you in Yosemite — the valley would not be the same without you. My girls cannot leave here till the schools close, about June 20, so we shall not get into the valley much before July first; but if you have a good winter, with plenty of snow, that will do. We shall stay as long as we like. George says he and Carrie can go, and I hope Sloots can. It is likely that Neale, my publisher, will be of my party. I shall hope to visit your mine afterward.

* * *

My health, which was pretty bad for weeks after returning from Sag Harbor, is restored, and I was never so young in all my life.

Here's wishing you and Carlt plenty of meat on the bone that the new year may fling to you.

Affectionately,

AMBROSE.

෨෬ ෨෬ ෨෬

Washington, D. C.,
February 14,
1912. DEAR GEORGE,

I'm a long time noticing your letter of January fifth, chiefly because, like Teddy, "I have nothing to say." There's this difference atwixt him and me — I could say something if I tried.

* * * I'm hoping that you are at work and doing something worth while, though I see nothing of yours. Battle against the encroaching abalone should not engage all your powers. That spearing salmon at night interests me, though doubtless the "season" will be over before I visit Carmel.

Bear Yosemite in mind for latter part of June, and use influence with Lora and Grizzly, even if Carlt should be inhumed in his mine.

We've had about seven weeks of snow and ice, the mercury around the zero mark most of the time. Once it was 13 below. You'd not care for that sort of thing, I fancy. Indeed, I'm a bit fatigued of it myself, and on Saturday next, God willing, shall put out my prow to sea and bring up, I hope, in Bermuda, not, of course, to remain long.

You did not send me the Weininger article on "Sex and Character" — I mean the extract that you thought like some of my stuff.

* * *

Sincerely yours,

AMBROSE BIERCE.

DEAR GEORGE,

I did not go to Bermuda; so I'm not "back." But I did go to Richmond, a city whose tragic and pathetic history, of which one is reminded by everything that one sees there, always gets on to my nerves with a particular dejection. True, the history is some fifty years old, but it is always with me when I'm there, making solemn eyes at me.

Washington, D. C., April 25, 1912.

You're right about "this season in the East." It has indeed been penetential. For the first time I am thoroughly disgusted and half-minded to stay in California when I go — a land where every prospect pleases, and only labor unions, progressives, suffragettes (and socialists) are vile. No, I don't think I could stand California, though I'm still in the mind to visit it in June. I shall be sorry to miss Carrie at Carmel, but hope to have the two of you on some excursion or camping trip. We *want* to go to Yosemite, which the girls have not seen, but if there's no water there it may not be advisable. Guess we'll have to let you natives decide. How would the Big Trees do as a substitute?

* * *

Girls is pizen, but not necessarily fatal. I've taken 'em in large doses all my life, and suffered pangs enough to equip a number of small Hells, but never has one of them paralyzed the inner working man. * * * But I'm not a poet. Moreover, as I've not yet put off my armor I oughtn't to boast.

So — you've subscribed for the Collected Works. Good! that is what you ought to have done a long time ago. It is what every personal friend of mine ought to have done, for all profess admiration of my work in literature. It is what I was fool enough to permit my publisher to think that many of them would do. How many do you guess have done so? I'll leave you guessing. God help the man with many friends, for *they* will not. My royalties on the sets sold to my friends are less than one-fourth of my outlay in free sets for other friends. Tell me not in cheerful numbers of the value and sincerity of friendships.

* * *

There! I've discharged my bosom of that perilous stuff and shall take a drink. Here's to you.

Sincerely yours,

AMBROSE BIERCE.

⋆⋆⋆

Washington, D. C.,
June 5,
1912.

DEAR GEORGE,

* * *

Thank you for the poems, which I've not had the time to consider — being disgracefully busy in order to get away. I don't altogether share your reverence for Browning, but the primacy of your verses on him over the others printed on the same page is almost startling. * * *

Of course it's all nonsense about the waning of your power — though thinking it so might make it so. My notion is that you've only *begun* to do things. But I wish you'd go back to your chain in your uncle's office. I'm no believer in adversity and privation as a spur to Pegasus. They are oftener a "hopple." The "meagre, muse-rid mope, adust and thin" will commonly do better work when tucked out with three square meals a day, and having the sure and certain hope of their continuance.

* * *

I'm expecting to arrive in Oakland (Key Route Inn, probably) late in the evening of the 22d of this month and dine at Carlt's on the 24th — my birthday. Anyhow, I've invited myself, though it is possible they may be away on their vacation. Carlt has promised to try to get his "leave" changed to a later date than the one he's booked for.

* * *

Sincerely yours,

AMBROSE BIERCE.

P. S. — Just learned that we can not leave here until the 19th — which will bring me into San Francisco on the 26th. Birthday dinner served in diner — last call!

I've *read* the Browning poem and I now know why there was a Browning. Providence foresaw you and prepared him for you — blessed be Providence! * * *

Mrs. Havens asks me to come to them at Sag Harbor — and shouldn't I like to! * * * Sure the song of the Sag Harbor frog would be music to me — as would that of the indigenous duckling.

ᔓ ᔓ ᔓ

MY DEAR MR. CAHILL,

I thank you for the article from *The Argonaut*, and am glad to get it for a special reason, as it gives me your address and thereby enables me to explain something.

When, several years ago, you sent me a similar article I took it to the editor of The National Geographical Magazine (I am a member of the Society that issues it) and suggested its publication. I left it with him and hearing nothing about it for several months called at his office *twice* for an answer, and for the copy if publication was refused. The copy had been "mislaid" — lost, apparently — and I never obtained it. Meantime, either I had "mislaid" your address, or it was only on the copy. So I was unable to write you. Indirectly, afterward, I heard that you had left California for parts to me unknown.

The Army and Navy Club, Washington, D. C., December 19, 1912.

Twice since then I have been in San Francisco, but confess that I did not think of the matter.

Cahill's projection* is indubitably the right one, but you are "up against" the ages and will be a long time dead before it finds favor, or I'm no true pessimist.

Sincerely yours,

AMBROSE BIERCE.

ᎧᎧ ᎧᎧ ᎧᎧ

The Olympia Apartments, Washington, D. C., January 17, 1913.

MY DEAR RUTH,

It's "too bad" that I couldn't remain in Oakland and Berkeley another month to welcome you, but I fear it will "have to go at that," for I've no expectation of ever seeing California again. I like the country as well as ever, but I *don't* like the rule of labor unions, the grafters and the suffragettes. So far as I am concerned they may stew in their own juice; I shall not offer myself as an ingredient.

It is pleasant to know that you are all well, including Johnny, poor little chap.

You are right to study philology and rhetoric. Surely there must be *some* provision for your need — a university where one cannot learn one's own language would be a funny university.

I think your "Mr. Wells" who gave a course of lectures on essay writing may be my friend Wells Drury, of Berkeley. If so, mention me to him and he will advise you what to do.

Another good friend of mine, whom, however I did not succeed in seeing during either of my visits to California, is W. C. Morrow, who is a professional teacher of writing and himself a splendid writer. He could help you. He lives in San Francisco, but I think has a class in Oakland. I don't

*The Butterfly Map of the World.

know his address; you'll find it in the directory. He used to write stories splendidly tragic, but I'm told he now teaches the "happy ending," in which he is right — commercially — but disgusting. I can cordially recommend him.

Keep up your German and French of course. If your English (your mother speech) is so defective, think what *they* must be.

I'll think of some books that will be helpful to you in your English. Meantime send me anything that you care to that you write. It will at least show me what progress you make.

I'm returning some (all, I think) of your sketches. Don't destroy them — yet. Maybe some day you'll find them worth rewriting.   My love to you all.

AMBROSE BIERCE.

❧ ❧ ❧

DEAR MR. CAHILL,

It is pleasant to know that you are not easily discouraged by the croaking of such ravens as I, and I confess that the matter of the "civic centre" supplies some reason to hope for prosperity to the Cahill projection — which (another croak) will doubtless bear some other man's name, probably Hayford's or Woodward's.

The Olympia, Euclid and 14th Sts., Washington, D. C., January 20, 1913.

I sent the "Argonaut" article to my friend Dr. Franklin, of Schenectady, a "scientific gent" of some note, but have heard nothing from him.

I'm returning the "Chronicle" article, which I found interesting. If I were not a writer without an "organ" I'd have a say about that projection. For near four years I've been out of the newspaper game — a mere compiler of my collected works in twelve volumes — and shall probably never "sit into the game" again, being seventy years old. My work is finished, and so am I.

Luck to you in the new year, and in many to follow.

Sincerely yours,

AMBROSE BIERCE.

❧ ❧ ❧

The Olympia
Apartments,
Washington, D. C.
I prefer to get my
letters at this address.
Make a memorandum
of it.
January 28,
1913.

DEAR LORA,

I have been searching for your letter of long ago, fearing it contained something that I should have replied to. But I don't find it; so I make the convenient assumption that it did not.

I'd like to hear from you, however unworthy I am to do so, for I want to know if you and Carlt have still a hope of going mining. Pray God you do, if there's a half-chance of success; for success in the service of the Government is failure.

Winter here is two-thirds gone and we have not had a cold day, and only one little dash of snow — on Christmas eve. Can California beat that? I'm told it's as cold there as in Greenland.

Tell me about yourself — your health since the operation — how it has affected you — all about you. My own health is excellent; I'm equal to any number of Carlt's toddies. By the way, Blanche has made me a co-defendant with you in the crime (once upon a time) of taking a drop too much. I plead not guilty — how do *you* plead? Sloots, at least, would acquit us on the ground of inability — that one *can't* take too much. * * * Affectionately, your avuncular,

AMBROSE.

❧ ❧ ❧

Washington, D. C.,
March 20,
1913.

DEAR RUTH,

I'm returning your little sketches with a few markings which are to be regarded (or disregarded) as mere suggestions. I made them in pencil, so that you can erase them if you don't approve. Of course I should make many more if I could have you before me so that I could explain *why*; in this way I can help you but little. You'll observe that I have made quite a slaughter of some of the adjectives in some of your sentences — you will doubtless slaughter some in others. Nearly all young writers use too many adjectives. Indeed, moderation and skill in the use of adjectives are about the last things a good writer learns. Don't use those that are connoted by the nouns; and rather than have all the nouns, or nearly all, in a sentence outfitted with them it is better to make separate sentences for some of those desired.

In your sketch "Triumph" I would not name the "hero" of the piece. To do so not only makes the sketch commonplace, but it logically requires you to name his victim too, and her offense; in brief, it commits you to a *story*.

A famous writer (perhaps Holmes or Thackeray — I don't remember) once advised a young writer to cut all the passages that he thought particularly good. Your taste I think is past the need of so heroic treatment as that, but the advice may be profitably borne in memory whenever you are in doubt, if ever you are. And sometimes you will be.

I think I know what Mr. Morrow meant by saying that your characters are not "humanly significant." He means that they are not such persons as one meets in everyday life — not "types." I confess that I never could see why one's characters *should* be. The exceptional — even "abnormal" — person seems to me the more interesting, but I must warn you that he will not seem so to an editor. Nor to an editor will the tragic element seem so good as the cheerful — the sombre denouement as the "happy ending." One must have a pretty firm reputation as a writer to "send in" a tragic or supernatural tale with any hope of its acceptance. The average mind (for which editors purvey, and mostly possess) dislikes, or thinks it dislikes, any literature that is not "sunny." True, tragedy holds the highest and most permanent place in the world's literature and art, but it has the divvel's own time getting to it. For immediate popularity (if one cares for it) one must write pleasant things; though one may put in here and there a bit of pathos.

I think well of these two manuscripts, but doubt if you can get them into any of our magazines — if you want to. As to that, nobody can help you. About the only good quality that a magazine editor commonly has is his firm reliance on the infallibility of his own judgment. It is an honest error, and it enables him to mull through somehow with a certain kind of consistency. The only way to get a footing with him is to send him what you think he wants, not what you think he ought to want — and keep sending. But perhaps you do not care for the magazines.

I note a great improvement in your style — probably no more than was to be expected of your better age, but a distinct improvement. It is a matter of regret with me that I have not the training of you; we should see what would come of it. You certainly have no reason for discouragement. But if you are to be a writer you must "cut out" the dances and the teas (a little of the theater may be allowed) and *work* right heartily. The way of the good writer is no primrose path.

No, I have not read the poems of Service. What do I think of Edith Wharton? Just what Pollard thought — see *Their Day in Court*, which I think you have.

I fear you have the wanderlust incurably. I never had it

bad, and have less of it now than ever before. I shall not see California again.

My love to all your family goes with this, and to you all that you will have.   AMBROSE BIERCE.

ϿϾ ϿϾ ϿϾ

EDITOR "LANTERN,"*

Will I tell you what I think of your magazine? Sure I will. It has thirty-six pages of reading matter.

Seventeen are given to the biography of a musician, — German, dead.

Four to the mother of a theologian, — German, peasant-wench, dead.

(The mag. is published in America, to-day.)

Five pages about Eugene Field's ancestors. All dead.

$17+4+5=26.$

$36-26=10.$

Two pages about Ella Wheeler Wilcox.

Three-fourths page about a bad poet and his indifference to — German.

Two pages of his poetry.

$2+\frac{3}{4}+2=4\frac{3}{4}.$

$10-4\frac{3}{4}=5\frac{1}{4}.$ Not enough to criticise.

What your magazine needs is an editor — presumably older, preferably American, and indubitably alive. At least awake. It is your inning.   Sincerely yours,

AMBROSE BIERCE.

The Army and
Navy Club,
Washington, D. C.,
May 22,
1913.

ϿϾ ϿϾ ϿϾ

MY DEAR LORA,

You were so long in replying to my letter of the century before last, and as your letter is not really a reply to any-

Washington, D. C.,
May 31,
1913.

*The editor was Curtis J. Kirch ("Guido Bruno") and the weekly had a brief career in Chicago. It was the forerunner of the many Bruno weeklies and monthlies, later published from other cities.

thing in mine, that I fancy you did not get it. I don't recol-lect, for example, that you ever acknowledged receipt of little pictures of myself, though maybe you did — I only hope you got them. The photographs that you send are very interesting. One of them makes me thirsty — the one of that fountainhead of good booze, your kitchen sink.

What you say of the mine and how you are to be housed there pleases me mightily. That's how I should like to live, and mining is what I should like again to do. Pray God you be not disappointed.

Alas, I cannot even join you during Carlt's vacation, for the mountain ramble. Please "go slow" in your goating this year. I *think* you are better fitted for it than ever be-fore, but you'd better ask your surgeon about that. By the way, do you know that since women took to athletics their peculiar disorders have increased about fifty per cent? You can't make men of women. The truth is, they've taken to walking on their hind legs a few centuries too soon. Their in'ards have not learned how to suspend the law of gravity. Add the jolts of athletics and — there you are.

I wish I could be with you at Monte Sano—or anywhere. Love to Carlt and Sloots. Affectionately,   AMBROSE.

ॐ ॐ ॐ

Washington, D. C.,   DEAR LORA,
September 10,   Your letter was forwarded to me in New York, whence I
1913.   have just returned. I fancy you had a more satisfactory outing than I. I never heard of the Big Sur river nor of "Arbolado." But I'm glad you went there, for I'm hearing so much about Hetch Hetchy that I'm tired of it. I'm help-ing the San Francisco crowd (a little) to "ruin" it.

* * *

I'm glad to know that you still expect to go to the mine.

Success or failure, it is better than the Mint, and you ought to live in the mountains where you can climb things whenever you want to.

Of course I know nothing of Neale's business — you'd better write to him if he has not filled your order. I suppose you know that volumes eleven and twelve are not included in the "set."

If you care to write to me again please do so at once as I am going away, probably to South America, but if we have a row with Mexico before I start I shall go there first. I want to see something going on. I've no notion of how long I shall remain away.

With love to Carlt and Sloots,   Affectionately,

AMBROSE.

❦ ❦ ❦

DEAR JOE,*

The reason that I did not answer your letter sooner is — I have been away (in New York) and did not have it with me. I suppose I shall not see your book for a long time, for I am going away and have no notion when I shall return. I expect to go to, perhaps across, South America — possibly via Mexico, if I can get through without being stood up against a wall and shot as a Gringo. But that is better than dying in bed, is it not? If Duc did not need you so badly I'd ask you to get your hat and come along. God bless and keep you.   * * *

Washington, D. C.,
September 10,
1913.

❦ ❦ ❦

DEAR JOE,

Thank you for the book. I thank you for your friendship — and much besides. This is to say good-by at the end of a pleasant correspondence in which your woman's preroga-

Washington, D. C.,
September 13,
1913.

*To Mrs. Josephine Clifford McCrackin, San Jose, California.

tive of having the last word is denied to you. Before I could receive it I shall be gone. But some time, somewhere, I hope to hear from you again. Yes, I shall go into Mexico with a pretty definite purpose, which, however, is not at present disclosable. You must try to forgive my obstinacy in not "perishing" where I am. I want to be where something worth while is going on, or where nothing whatever is going on. Most of what is going on in your own country is exceedingly distasteful to me.

Pray for me? Why, yes, dear — that will not harm either of us. I loathe religions, a Christian gives me qualms and a Catholic sets my teeth on edge, but pray for me just the same, for with all those faults upon your head (it's a nice head, too), I am pretty fond of you, I guess. May you live as long as you want to, and then pass smilingly into the darkness — the good, good darkness.

Devotedly your friend,
AMBROSE BIERCE.

߄߄ ߄߄ ߄߄

The Olympia,
Euclid Street,
Washington, D. C.,
October 1,
1913.

DEAR LORA,

I go away tomorrow for a long time, so this is only to say good-bye. I think there is nothing else worth saying; *therefore* you will naturally expect a long letter. What an intolerable world this would be if we said nothing but what is worth saying! And did nothing foolish — like going into Mexico and South America.

I'm hoping that you will go to the mine soon. You must hunger and thirst for the mountains — Carlt likewise. So do I. Civilization be dinged! — it is the mountains and the desert for me.

Good-bye — if you hear of my being stood up against a Mexican stone wall and shot to rags please know that I think that a pretty good way to depart this life. It beats old age, disease, or falling down the cellar stairs. To be a Gringo in Mexico — ah, that is euthanasia!

With love to Carlt, affectionately yours,   AMBROSE.

⁂

My DEAR LORA,

I think I owe you a letter, and probably this is my only chance to pay up for a long time. For more than a month I have been rambling about the country, visiting my old battlefields, passing a few days in New Orleans, a week in San Antonio, and so forth. I turned up here this morning. There is a good deal of fighting going on over on the Mexican side of the Rio Grande, but I hold to my intention to go into Mexico if I can. In the character of "innocent bystander" I ought to be fairly safe if I don't have too much money on me, don't you think? My eventual destination is South America, but probably I shall not get there this year.

Sloots writes me that you and Carlt still expect to go to the mine, as I hope you will.

The Cowdens expect to live somewhere in California soon, I believe. They seem to be well, prosperous and cheerful.

With love to Carlt and Sloots, I am affectionately yours,
AMBROSE.

P. S. You need not believe *all* that these newspapers say of me and my purposes. I had to tell them *something*.

Laredo, Texas, November 6, 1913.

⁂

DEAR LORA,

I wrote you yesterday at San Antonio, but dated the letter here and today, expecting to bring the letter and mail it here. That's because I did not know if I would have time

Laredo, Texas, November 6, 1913.

to write it here. Unfortunately, I forgot and posted it, with other letters, where it was written. Thus does man's guile come to naught!

Well, I'm here, anyhow, and have time to explain.

Laredo was a Mexican city before it was an American. It is Mexican now, five to one. Nuevo Laredo, opposite, is held by the Huertistas and Americans don't go over there. In fact a guard on the bridge will not let them. So those that sneak across have to wade (which can be done almost anywhere) and go at night.

I shall not be here long enough to hear from you, and don't know where I shall be next. Guess it doesn't matter much.   Adios,

                                                    AMBROSE.

Extracts from Letters

You are right too — dead right about the poetry of Social-ism; and you might have added the poetry of wailing about the woes of the poor generally. Only the second- and the third-raters write it — except "incidentally." You don't find the big fellows sniveling over that particular shadow-side of Nature. Yet not only are the poor always with us, they always *were* with us, and their state was worse in the times of Homer, Virgil, Shakspeare, Milton and the others than in the days of Morris and Markham.

༄ ༄ ༄

But what's the use? I have long despaired of convincing poets and artists of anything, even that white is not black. I'm convinced that all you chaps ought to have a world to yourselves, where two and two make whatever you prefer that it *should* make, and cause and effect are remoulded "more nearly to the heart's desire." And then I suppose I'd want to go and live there too.

༄ ༄ ༄

Did you ever know so poor satire to make so great a row as that of Watson? Compared with certain other verses against particular women — Byron's "Born in a garret, in a kitchen bred"; even my ówn skit entitled "Mad" (pardon my modesty) it is infantile. What an interesting book might be made of such "attacks" on women! But Watson is the only one of us, so far as I remember, who has had the caddishness to *name* the victim.

Have you seen Percival Pollard's "Their Day in Court"? It is amusing, clever — and more. He has a whole chapter on me, "a lot" about Gertrude Atherton, and much else that is interesting. And he skins alive certain popular gods and goddesses of the day, and is "monstrous naughty."

As to * * * 's own character I do not see what that has to do with his criticism of London. If only the impeccable delivered judgment no judgment would ever be delivered. All men could do as they please, without reproof or dissent. I wish you would take your heart out of your head, old man. The best heart makes a bad head if housed there.

The friends that warned you against the precarious nature of my friendship were right. To hold my regard one must fulfil hard conditions — hard if one is not what one should be; easy if one is. I have, indeed, a habit of calmly considering the character of a man with whom I have fallen into any intimacy and, whether I have any grievance against him or not, informing him by letter that I no longer desire his acquaintance. This, I do after deciding that he is not truthful, candid, without conceit, and so forth — in brief, honorable. If any one is conscious that he is not in all respects worthy of my friendship he would better not cultivate it, for assuredly no one can long conceal his true character from an observant student of it. Yes, my friendship is a precarious possession. It grows more so the longer I live, and the less I feel the need of a multitude of friends. So, if in your heart you are conscious of being any of the things which you accuse *me* of being, or anything else equally objectionable (to *me*) I can only advise you to drop me before I drop you.

Certainly you have an undoubted right to your opinion of my ability, my attainments and my standing. If you choose to publish a censorious judgment of these matters, do so by all means: I don't think I ever cared a cent for what was printed about me, except as it supplied me with welcome material for my pen. One may presumably have a "sense of duty to the public," and the like. But convincing one person (one at a time) of one's friend's deficiencies is hardly worth while, and is to be judged differently. It comes under another rule. * * *

Maybe, as you say, my work lacks "soul," but my life does not, as a man's life is the man. Personally, I hold that sentiment has a place in this world, and that loyalty to a friend is not inferior as a characteristic to correctness of literary judgment. If there is a heaven I think it is more valued there. If Mr. * * * (your publisher as well as mine) had considered you a Homer, a Goethe or a Shakspeare a team of horses could not have drawn from *me* the expression of a lower estimate. And let me tell you that if you are going through life as a mere thinking machine, ignoring the generous promptings of the heart, sacrificing it to the brain, you will have a hard row to hoe, and the outcome, when you survey it from the vantage ground of age, will not please you. You seem to me to be beginning rather badly, as regards both your fortune and your peace of mind.

* * *

I saw * * * every day while in New York, and he does not

know that I feel the slightest resentment toward you, nor do I know it myself. So far as he knows, or is likely to know (unless you will have it otherwise) you and I are the best of friends, or rather, I am the best of friends to you. And I guess that is so. I could no more hate you for your disposition and character than I could for your hump if you had one. You are as Nature has made you, and your defects, whether they are great or small, are your misfortunes. I would remove them if I could, but I know that I cannot, for one of them is inability to discern the others, even when they are pointed out.

I must commend your candor in one thing. You confirm * * * words in saying that you commented on "my seeming lack of sympathy with certain modern masters," which you attribute to my not having read them. That is a conclusion to which a low order of mind in sympathy with the "modern masters" naturally jumps, but it is hardly worthy of a man of your brains. It is like your former lofty assumption that I had not read some ten or twelve philosophers, naming them, nearly all of whom I had read, and laughed at, before you were born. In fact, one of your most conspicuous characteristics is the assumption that what a a man who does not care to "talk shop" does not speak of, and vaunt his knowledge of, he does not know. I once thought this a boyish fault, but you are no longer a boy. Your "modern masters" are Ibsen and Shaw, with both of whose works and ways I am thoroughly familiar, and both of whom I think very small men — pets of the drawing-room and gods of the hour. No, I am not an "up to date" critic, thank God. I am not a literary critic at all, and never, or very seldom, have gone into that field except in pursuance of a personal object — to help a good writer (who is commonly a friend) —maybe you can recall such instances — or laugh at a fool. Surely you do not consider my work in the Cosmopolitan (mere badinage and chaff, the only kind of stuff that the magazine wants from me, or will print) essays in literary criticism. It has never occurred to me to look upon myself as a literary critic; if you *must* prick my bubble please to observe that it contains more of your breath than of mine. Yet you have sometimes seemed to value, I thought, some of my notions about even poetry. * * *

Perhaps I am unfortunate in the matter of keeping friends; I know, and have abundant reason to know, that you are at least equally luckless in the matter of making them. I could put my finger on the very qualities in you that make you so, and the best service that I could do you would be to point them out and take the consequences. That is to say, it would serve you many years hence; at present you are like Carlyle's "Mankind"; you "refuse to be served." You only consent to be enraged.

I bear you no ill will, shall watch your career in letters with friendly solicitude — have, in fact, just sent to the * * * a most appreciative paragraph about your book, which may or may not commend itself to the editor; most of what I write does not. I hope to do a little, now and then, to further your success in letters. I wish you were different (and that is the harshest criticism that I ever uttered of you except to yourself) and wish it for your sake more than for mine. I am older than you and probably more "acquainted with grief" — the grief of disappointment and disillusion. If in the future you are convinced that you have become different, and I am still living, my welcoming hand awaits you. And when I forgive I forgive all over, even the new offence.

Miller undoubtedly is sincere in his praise of you, for with all his faults and follies he is always generous and usually over generous to other poets. There's nothing little and mean in him. Sing ho for Joaquin!

∂☙ ∂☙ ∂☙

If I "made you famous" please remember that you were guilty of contributory negligence by meriting the fame. "Eternal vigilance" is the price of its permanence. Don't loaf on your job. ∂☙ ∂☙ ∂☙

I have told her of a certain "enchanted forest" hereabout to which I feel myself sometimes strongly drawn as a fitting place to lay down "my weary body and my head." (Perhaps you remember your Swinburne:

> "Ah yet, would God this flesh of mine might be
> Where air might wash and long leaves cover me!
> Ah yet, would God that roots and stems were bred
> Out of my weary body and my head.")

The element of enchantment in that forest is supplied by my wandering and dreaming in it forty-one years ago when I was a-soldiering and there were new things under a new sun. It is miles away, but from a near-by summit I can overlook the entire region — ridge beyond ridge, parted by purple valleys full of sleep. Unlike me, it has not visibly altered in all these years, except that I miss, here and there, a thin blue ghost of smoke from an enemy's camp. Can you guess my feelings when I view this Dream-land — my Realm of Adventure, inhabited by memories that beckon me from every valley? I shall go; I shall retrace my old routes and lines of march; stand in my old camps; inspect my battlefields to see that all is right and undisturbed. I shall go to the Enchanted Forest.